Little Kid Paper Plate Crafts

The Definitive Guide to Creating Great Paper Plate Projects for Kids 2 and Up

By Chris Yates

Lusie Ltd. In cooperation with

KidCraftsMagazine.com
FreeKidCrafts.com

Copyright © 2012 by Lusie Ltd.

All Rights Reserved.

Templates and craft instruction pages may be reproduced for individual sue or classroom use only, not for commercial resale. No portion of this publication may be reproduced for storage in a retrieval system, or transmitted in any form or by any means, electronic, mechanical, recording, etc., without the written permission of the publisher. Reproduction of these materials for an entire school, school system, or day care is strictly prohibited. Reproduction of these materials on websites, blogs, and newsletters is strictly prohibited.

Little Kids series is written, illustrated, and edited by Lusie Ltd.

NOTICE: The information contained in this book is true, complete, and accurate to the best of our knowledge. All recommendations and suggestions are made without any guarantees on the part of the author or publisher. The author and publisher disclaim all liability incurred in conjunction with the use of this information and encourage adult supervision of young children at all times.

"Some people weave burlap into the fabric of our lives, and some weave gold thread. Both contribute to make the whole picture beautiful and unique."
- Anonymous

This book is dedicated to all those who weave gold thread into the lives of children every day.

Contents

Contents 5
Forward 9
A Few Notes Before We Start… 13
   How This Book Is Organized 14
   A Few Ground Rules… 16
   Preparation Is Golden… 17
A Note On Safety… 19
Heads and Other Round Things… 21
   The Basics… 21
   Front or Back? 23
   Color 24
   Features 25
   Feature Placement 27
   Add On's 27
   Non-Head Uses 30
   Koala 31
   Rabbit 32
   Mouse 33
   Dog 34
   Simple Cat 35
   Duck 36
   Elephant 37
   Lion 38
   Jack-o-Lantern 39
   Clown 40
   Simple Sun 41
   Award 42
   Clock 43
   Winter Scene 43
   Picture Frame 45
   Pizza 46
   Simple Ladybug 47
   Wormy Apple 48

Templates For Heads and Other Round Things 49

Flat Animals… 55

    The Low-Down on Flat Animals… 57

    Creating Flat Animals 57

    Flat Cat 59

    Flat Frog 60

    Turkey 61

    Flat Duck 62

    Turtle 63

    Flat Sheep 64

    Tropical Fish 65

    Flat Cow 66

    Flat Leopard 67

    Crab 68

    Raccoon 69

Multiple Plate Projects… 77

    Caterpillar 81

    Tired Lion 82

    Funny Flat Frog 83

    Apple Shaker 86

    Hand Puppet Puppy 88

    Silly Hat 89

    Quacking Duck 92

Folding, Bending, & Cutting… 93

    Now For The Fun Stuff… 95

    Fall Wreath 101

    Christmas Bow Basket 103

    Purple Brontosaurus 104

    Sun Baby 105

    Owl 108

    Stegosaurus 110

    Shapes Mobile 111

    Spiral Easter Egg Mobile 113

    Fish Bowl 114

    Winged Ladybug 115

    Simple Summer Flower 116

- Sandy Snake 117
- Monster Mask 118
- May Basket 119
- Queen Of Summer Crown 120
- Door Pocket 121

Advanced Techniques and Challenging Projects 123
- Where Do You Go From Here… 123
- Funny Flat Elephant 126
- Caged Circus Animal 127
- Sleepy Pig 130
- Port Hole to the Ocean Floor 132
- Crazy Hair People 133
- Woven Plate 135
- Stuffed Angelfish 136
- Prickly Cactus 137
- Rocking on the Sea 140

Forward

Writing this book has been a very personal experience for me. I began this book and my own website out of sheer disappointment in what was available to parents, preschool teachers, daycare workers, and other people who work with small children. After searching through every online resource I could find and buying just about every book ever written on crafting with younger children, I walked away with the feeling that this area of kids' crafts has been severely overlooked. Most of what I found was either too old for my kids, the same or reworked projects on free sites, or completely commercialized.

Sure, you can find a wealth of books on crafting with school age children. In fact, some of the books for this age group are absolutely beautiful and have original content, but let me ask you:

How many books or other resources do you find for Little Kids?

I don't mean elementary school kids, I mean toddlers and preschoolers. You'll find many books that claim to be for children ages 2 or 3 to 6, but I can tell you from my own experience that they are really aimed at the 5 and 6 year olds. I've bought many of these books only to be disappointed to find that they had 2 or 3 crafts, out of 50 or more, that were projects that my 3 year old could do.

In fairness, crafting with toddlers and preschoolers does come with its own set of challenges. At this age kids have just about no attention span, have to be constantly monitored, often don't have any concept of what they are supposed to be making, and are only capable of very simple tasks.

Challenging, but not impossible...

Most craft books that claim to be for toddlers and preschoolers have crafts that require an adult to do so much project assembly that it becomes more an adult project than a child's project. Don't get me wrong, some adult assistance is necessary for any craft project or activity that you do with Little Kids, but some of the crafts that I've seen and tried to do with my own children were so difficult or time consuming that my children lost interest within minutes.

Looking back, it's kind of funny to think that I'm trying to "help" them put their project together while they are entertaining themselves by finger painting my kitchen walls, the table, and themselves.

The second thing that really irritated me about Little Kid crafting is the lack of originality. I can't tell you how many books that I have purchased that had only a handful of original ideas, while the bulk of the book was dedicated to super-sized pictures and rehashed material available in 20 other books. In other words, they had very little substance.

There is a series of children's crafting books out on the market today (I don't think it would be right to name it.) that dedicates two pages to each craft idea or project. On first glance, this may not seem like a lot, (most of my projects take two pages too) but here's a reality check:

More than half of each of the two pages is taken up by unnecessary pictures - pictures that don't add to the value of the craft or its description.

After purchasing several books in the series, I discovered that many of the crafts were just about identical. Here's some examples:

In one book there is a project that does apple prints with paint. The next book in the series does vegetable prints.

In the same book there is a "Recycling Sculpture" using blocks of Styrofoam and later there is a "Wood Sculpture" using scrap pieces of wood. Then of course there are other "original" projects like an oatmeal container drum, woven berry baskets, cardboard box buildings, a king's crown, and the infamous clothespin butterfly.

If all this regurgitated garbage weren't enough, many of the rest of the projects are far too old for little hands. For example: shred crayons with a potato peeler onto a piece of paper, fold it over and put an iron on it to melt the crayons.

Now, what part of this project do you want your 2 or 3 year old to do? Should they handle the sharp potato peeler or the hot iron?

Believe it or not, I bought several books similar to the one described above for $12.95 each - What a waste of money!

Then I started my online search for more crafting inspiration with my own children. I've looked at hundreds of websites over the course of the last few years. Most of them have three things in common:

- They are full of banner ads, pop-ups, and false recommendations for products that are either unrelated to kid crafting or products that the site owners have obviously never used themselves.

- They contain only a handful of the same old projects you've seen a thousand times interspersed among the advertisements.

- They are so poorly organized and difficult to browse or search that you can't find anything.

These are the things that prompted me to build my own websites dedicated to crafting with kids. You've probably already visited it if you're reading this book. It's at:

www.FreeKidCrafts.com
www.KidCraftsMagazine.com

My sites have very little advertising on them, and anything that is advertised on the sites are for products that I have used, or my children have used. I have used a lot of software and technology on the website to make it easy to browse the crafts and to search for particular craft ideas. Lastly, I continuously add new crafts and activities to the sites... and not just the same ideas you see all over the internet. I'm proud of the sites and I think I've done it right. They are the kind of websites that I would like to visit.

And so now in this second edition, after selling thousands of copies in simple ebook format, I'm finally able to offer Little Kid Crafts For All Seasons in a bound book (physical edition) as well as a Kindle edition.
The craft ideas in this book are not available on my site and they aren't in any of my other books. These are my own original ideas specifically written for this book - and I've got pages of handwritten notes to prove it!

It is my sincerest wish that you find it a useful part of your kid crafting library and that it shines as an example of how children's crafting books should be written.

Best Wishes and Happy Little Kid Crafting!

Chris Yates

A Few Notes Before We Start…

Many of you who have purchased my other books or visited my web site already know that I have my own philosophy about crafting with Little Kids. It can be tremendous fun for you and your child when you pick age-appropriate activities, prepare all the materials in advance, and dedicate your time to that crafting period. Crafting can be frustrating, maddening, and a total pain in the neck if you don't.

When it comes to crafting with Little Kids, it is less important that the craft looks like what it's supposed to and more important that it provides a good creative outlet for the child.

Who cares if a dog's ears are purple and his nose is green?

Who says a duck can't be pink?

Give your child the freedom to do it their way. That's the most important gift you can give your child when you craft with them.

How This Book Is Organized

I've taken a very different approach in this book. It is unlike any other children's craft book you are likely to encounter and it is definitely more comprehensive than any other paper plate craft book that exists on the market today.

The book is divided into different sections that deal with a specific way to use a paper plate. For example, paper plates are used as the head of a large variety of animals and people. There really wouldn't be much point in telling you how to make every different kind of animal I can think of. That would be ridiculous!

Instead, I've taken a different approach. I show you how to create the basic paper plate animal and then I show you how you can adapt the craft into other animals by changing the color, ears, nose, mouth, etc.

Now you have a book that will allow you to create an infinite number of animals!

I've created a different section of the book for every way I can think of to use a basic paper plate. In addition, you'll notice that the sections of the book basically proceed with increasing levels of difficulty. This will help you to find a project that's appropriate to your child's skill level instead of just their age.

This book will actually grow with your child!

Each section of the book also contains examples of the unique crafts that I've created with my own children using paper plates. I'm not just talking about pictures, I'm talking about full project sheets for my own unique paper plate crafts. This should serve to give you the inspiration to experiment with your own craft ideas.

Lastly, each section contains templates for craft projects that are appropriate to that section. You can use these templates as they are or adapt them to another craft idea. If you don't know how to draw a basic animal ear or a frog's leg, don't worry. I've done it for you.

I've made paper plate crafting as easy as I can so you and your child can get the most out of it.

A Few Ground Rules...

All right, "ground rules" probably isn't the right way to say it, but here are a few things you need to know about my instructions in this book.

I often talk about stapling different components together instead of gluing them. There are a couple of reasons.

First of all, stapling is so fast. If you are helping a young child put a project together, they are going to quickly lose interest if you are gluing pieces together. Stapling a project together is quick and allows them to immediately play with their creation. If it's a part of the project that a parent has to help assemble, then I'll probably recommend stapling. If it's something that a child can do unassisted, then use the glue.

Occasionally, I call for hot glue. This is also a parent-only job. I only call for hot glue on the parts of a project that require some parental assistance. If you are working with a little older child that can assemble everything themselves, then let them use white glue or a glue stick instead.

Speaking of glue sticks, I'm a big fan of them. When I am crafting with my own children, we use glue sticks whenever possible. They are less likely to wrinkle or discolor paper and they are a lot less messy than ordinary white household glue.

When I refer to craft sticks, this is what I mean:

Large Craft Stick = Tongue Depressor

Small Craft Stick = Popsicle Stick

When I refer to a paper plate, I generally mean a cheap 9 inch paper plate that doesn't have any wax coating on it. These are the kind of paper plates that you get a couple of hundred plates for a dollar. I will specifically state that a heavy duty plate or an smaller plate is necessary if it is.

Preparation Is Golden...

Preparing your materials and your craft in advance is probably the most important factor in whether the craft time with your child is fun for you both or whether it is full of stress for you and leads to tears and frustration for your child.

Here are a few things to think about.

1. **If Possible, do the draft for yourself the night before you plan to do it with your child.**

   This serves two purposes. First of all, it gives you the opportunity to see what parts of the project may be difficult for your child to do, so you may want to change something in the project.

   Sometimes you will find that a particular idea just won't work with your child and you have to scrap it. Better to find out before you try to sit down with your child and do it.

2. **Gather all your materials before you sit down to craft.**

   This is a hugely important factor in a successful craft session with your child. If you have to keep popping up to get some supply needed for your project, you're probably going to come back to a disaster.

   Children have such short attention spans anyway, so if you make them wait while you go and get the next supply, they will either give up on the project entirely, or find something else to entertain themselves, like cutting their bangs or sprinkling glitter all over the floor.

Having everything assembled in advance, including covering your surface with newspaper, gathering smocks and protective clothing, and preparing cleanup materials like soap and water will make the entire craft project a stress free, fun, and memorable time for you and your child.

A Note On Safety...

I'm sure you are a very safety minded adult and you don't need me to give you a long song and dance about how to keep your kids safe during crafting. Having said that, I still want to mention a few things.

1. Don't walk away and leave a child unattended while crafting. There's all kinds of things that could happen to hurt them, not to mention destroying the craft area.

2. Don't let kids do parent jobs like stapling, hole punching, using hot glue, etc.

3. If you're using small objects like brads and buttons, don't let your child put them in their mouth. Small objects pose a choking hazard and should be monitored.

4. Only let children use child safety scissors to cut.

5. Only use non-toxic paints, crayons, markers, glue, etc.

6. Closely monitor kids around any object that is hot like a hot glue gun or oven. Little Kid skin burns easily.

Heads and Other Round Things...

The Basics...

You can create just about any kind of animal or person that you want with a paper plate. The round shape and size of a paper plate, not to mention the availability and the economical benefits, makes it a perfect starting point for a variety of craft projects.

When it comes to crafting with young children, paper plates are most often used as the head of an animal or person. Each one of these types of projects looks completely different, but I'm going to show you that you can create any kind of animal or person you want just by changing a few key components.

Front or Back?

One of the first things you have to decide when you want to create a paper plate object is whether the front or the back of the paper plate is the best for you to use.

In general, if you are creating a head of some kind, you'll want to use the back side of the paper plate. If you turn it over on a table, you'll notice that it bubbles up slightly.

The slightly convex shape helps to create a three dimensional effect that makes the head look more realistic to a child.

If on the other hand, you want to do a non-head project, you'll have to decide which side of the paper plate better suits your project. We'll talk more about non-head projects later in this section.

Color

Color plays a significant role in most craft projects, and paper plate crafts are no exception. If you're making a bear's head, you'll probably want to paint the back side of a paper plate brown to start out your craft. If you're making a pig, you'll probably want to paint the plate pink. If you're making a bunny, the plate probably won't get painted at all and remain white.

Often times, color will determine what kind of animal you are actually making. For example, you'll see below a picture of a cat and a picture of a tiger. If it weren't for the paint, how could you tell them apart?

You'll see as we progress through this section of the book that color is very important when it comes to paper plate crafting.

Features

Even more important than the color you paint your paper plate is the features that you put on your plate. By features, I mean the eyes, nose, mouth, ears, etc. An elephant just wouldn't look right without the ears, and a duck needs a bill.

The point here, however, is that some sets of features can do double duty. Take a look at the ears below.

When you look at this set of ears, can you tell if it is a bear, dog, panda, or lion? Of course not. It could be any of these animals.

Now, look at this nose...

What kind of nose is it?

And these eyes?

These eyes could belong to just about any animal you can think of. They could even be human. My point is that you can use the same set of features or combinations of features over and over again to make different kinds of animals. You want to make a cat?

Choose a pointy set of ears...

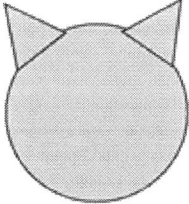

A triangle nose...

Some basic eyes...

Add some cheeks and a mouth...

Complete the project with a few whiskers... And now you have a complete cat.

Want to make this a tiger? Paint on stripes.

Want to make it a leopard? Paint on some spots.

Do you see where I'm going with this? This is so easy that anyone can plan out a great paper plate project that any 3 year old would love!

Feature Placement

Another important thing to consider as you are developing your own paper plate crafts is feature placement. Sometimes the features you choose to put on your plate are not as important as where you choose to put them.

A perfect example of this idea is a rabbit and his ears. If you put a set of basic rabbit ears on a paper plate sticking straight up in the air, then it definitely looks like a rabbit no matter what else you do to it.

If, however, you take those same basic rabbit ears and flop them down to the side of the plate...

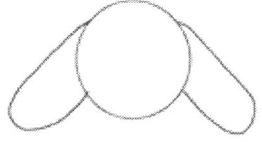 Suddenly your rabbit starts to look more like a floppy eared dog.

Some animals have their ear placement higher or lower than most, others have eyes that are closer or further apart. The best you can do when it comes to animals is to get a good animal book and create your paper plate project from the picture of the animal you want to do.

Add On's

Up until this point, I haven't really discussed whether the features in each project are drawn on or cut out of construction paper and glued on. I guess because it's both.

Ears most often have to be glued on, while facial features can be drawn or glued on. When I talk about add on's, I'm really talking about two different classes of add on's.

First there are things that you might glue onto a plate that could also be painted or drawn in. For example, a lion's mane could be painted or it could be cut out of construction paper and glued onto a plate.

The second type of add on that I'm referring to is the type of add on that's really not necessary to make the project.

For example, if you were making a bear and you chose to glue buttons on the eyes instead of drawing them in, that would be an add on.

Another example of an add on is a set of pipe cleaner glasses glued onto your paper plate person.

There are a ton of different objects that you can use as add on's for your projects:

buttons	beans
rice	sand
yarn	pom poms
pipe cleaners	feathers
ribbon	sequins
glitter	foam
shipping peanuts	cereal
tissue paper	cotton balls

There's probably a lot more add on's than I have listed here, but you get the idea. These types of materials can really add a lot to a project. Even if they really don't add too much to a project, they are fun for children to use and a good way to get more mileage out of a project.

Let me explain...

You could do several paper plate lions with your child throughout the year without either of you getting bored or feeling like you've repeated anything. Here's how it works:

1. The first lion you do is a basic one where you paint on the mane and then draw on all the features with a marker.

2. Several weeks later you do another lion, only this time, you paint the plate and then make all the parts out of construction paper. (ie. the mane, ears, eyes, etc.)

3. Several weeks later you make another paper plate lion. This time you paint the plate, draw on all the features, and then glue on pieces of yarn to make the mane.

I could keep coming up with new combinations of lion projects using yarn, buttons, construction paper, etc., but I think you get the idea. Add on's really help you get a lot of mileage out of one project idea.

Non-Head Uses

A lot of different kinds of objects can be made with a paper plate. Basically, if it's round, you can make it out of a paper plate. There's another section later on in the book about folding, bending and cutting paper plates to make particular objects, so I'm not going to discuss those kinds of projects at this point.

I'll give you some examples later on in this section, but non-head uses for a plate would be things like a clock face, a picture frame, a scene of some kind, a sun, apple, etc.

You can really let you imagination be your guide here.

Now... Let's see some paper plate project examples so you can start creating your own unique projects!

Koala

This is kind of an unusual animal to make, and one that most younger kids won't even recognize… But it presents a great opportunity to talk to your child about the animal, it's habitat, etc. You could even extend the project by doing it in conjunction with a zoo trip!

You'll Need:

- Eye and Nose Templates (at the end of this section)
- 9 Inch Paper Plate
- Gray Tempera Paint
- Paint Brush
- Gray Construction Paper
- White Construction Paper
- Black Marker
- Scissors
- Glue

Directions:

1. Paint the back side of a paper plate gray and let dry.

2. Tear 2 rectangles of gray paper measuring about 6 x 4 inches. Tear a second set of rectangles that are a little smaller than the first from white paper. Glue the white paper onto the gray paper to make the center of the ears. Glue the ears to the back side of the paper plate so that they stick out.

3. Print out or copy the eyes and nose for the koala and glue onto the plate.

4. Draw a mouth with marker.

Rabbit

Everybody loves making cute little bunnies, and it's so easy when you get to start with a paper plate. These are great for Easter, but can also be used at just about any time of year.

You'll Need:

- Rabbit Ear Templates (at the end of this section)
- 9 Inch Paper Plate
- Pink Construction Paper
- White Construction Paper
- Black Marker
- Scissors
- Glue

Directions:

1. Print out the rabbit ears on white construction paper.

2. Print out the inside of the rabbit ears on pink paper.

3. Cut out both sets of ears.

4. Glue each of the pink inner ears to the white outer ears. Glue the ears to the back side of the paper plate so that they stick up.

5. Print out or copy the general eyes at the end of this section and cut a triangle for a nose. Glue the eyes and nose onto the plate.

4. Draw a mouth and whiskers with a marker.

Mouse

You probably never thought about making a paper plate mouse, unless it's Mickey (which would be really easy to make if you want), but this is a super simple project kids will love.

You'll Need:

- Templates at the end of this section
- 9 Inch Paper Plate
- Brown Construction Paper
- Pink Construction Paper
- Brown Tempera Paint
- Paint Brush
- Scissors
- Black Marker
- Glue

Directions:

1. Print the mouse ears on brown construction paper. Cut out. Also cut out a smaller inner ear from pink construction paper, using the outer ear as a guide.

2. Glue the pink inner ear to the brown outer ear. Glue the ears to the back side of the paper plate so that they stick out from the plate.

3. Print out or copy the eyes and nose for the mouse, color (when appropriate), cut out, and glue onto the plate.

4. Draw a mouth, cheeks, and whiskers with a marker.

Dog

This is one of my favorite projects because it reminds me of a dog that my best friend owned.

Her name was Sadie... the dog, not the friend.

You'll Need:

- Dog Ear Template
- Paper Plate
- Brown Construction Paper
- Scissors
- Black Marker
- Glue

Directions:

1. Print out the Dog Ear Template on brown construction paper.

2. Cut out and glue onto the front of the paper plate.

3. Draw the facial features onto the paper plate with a black marker or use some of the basic "features" included in the templates area at the end of this section.

Simple Cat

Cats are always a crafting favorite for kids of all ages. There's just something about cats that's fun to make... Maybe it's the whiskers!

As we discussed earlier in the book, you can easily turn this basic cat into any animal in the cat family. Paint on stripes to make it a tiger or spots to make it a leopard.

You'll Need:

- Paper Plate
- Light Brown and Pink Construction Paper
- Light Brown Tempera Paint
- Paint Brush
- Scissors
- Black Marker
- Glue

Directions:

1. Paint the back side of a paper plate light brown. Let dry.

2. Cut 2 triangles out of construction paper to make the ears. Glue them onto the paper plate. Cut a smaller triangle out of pink paper and glue that on for a nose.

3. Draw the facial features shown below onto the paper plate with a black marker. Don't forget to draw the whiskers!

If you want to, you can also glue on pieces of string or pipe cleaners to make three dimensional whiskers instead of drawing them on.

Duck

I think this is a really fun project, not only because it uses that big, wide duck bill, but also because it includes a few feathers for three dimensional project.

You'll Need:

- Duck Bill Template
- Paper Plate
- Orange Construction Paper
- Yellow Tempera Paint
- Paint Brush
- Yellow Feathers
- Scissors
- Black Marker
- Glue Stick

Directions:

1. Paint the back side of the paper plate with the yellow tempera paint and let dry.

2. Print the Duck Bill Template onto orange construction paper. Cut out and glue onto the front of the paper plate.

3. Draw the eyes with a black marker. If you prefer, you can also print a set of general eyes from the template section and glue them onto the duck.

4. Glue a few yellow feathers to the top of the duck's head.

Elephant

This a great project that will definitely look like what it's supposed to when it's done. The best thing about this particular elephant is that there's a complete template available at the end of this section.

You'll Need:

- Elephant Template
- Paper Plate
- Gray and White Construction Paper
- Gray Tempera Paint
- Paint Brush
- Scissors
- Glue

Directions:

1. Paint the back side of paper plate gray. Let dry.

2. Print out the elephant's trunk and ears from the Elephant Template onto gray construction paper. Cut out.

3. Glue the ears onto the back of the plate, using the tabs. Glue the trunk onto the front of the paper plate.

4. Draw the eyes with a black marker or cut them out of white paper and glue on.

Lion

This is another one of those project that kids will really enjoy making. It's super simple and will look like a lion when it's finished. Plus it's really fun to tear the paper to make the mane!

You'll Need:

- Ear Template
- Paper Plate
- Light Brown Construction Paper
- Orange Construction Paper
- Light Brown or Yellow Tempera Paint
- Paint Brush
- Scissors
- Black Marker
- Glue

Directions:

1. Paint the back side of a paper plate light brown or yellow. Let dry completely.

2. Print out or trace the ears from the template section onto light brown construction paper. Cut out and glue onto the back of the paper plate so that they stick out.

3. Draw the eyes with a black marker or cut them out of white paper and glue on.

4. Create the mane by tearing paper into a circle that's slightly larger than the plate. Glue the unpainted side of the plate to the center of the paper.

Jack-o-Lantern

What Halloween would be complete without a paper plate jack-o-lantern? This project is fun and easy, but it's also great to do with older kids. All you have to do is let them create their own face design instead of using triangles.

You'll Need:

- Paper Plate
- Green and Black Construction Paper
- Orange Tempera Paint
- Paint Brush
- Scissors
- Glue

Directions:

1. Paint the back side of the paper plate orange. Let dry.

2. Cut out three triangles and a mouth shape from black construction paper. Glue on for the face.

3. Cut a stem shape out of green construction paper and glue onto the back side of paper plate so that it sticks up from top of plate.

Clown

Kids enjoy this project because they can use bright colors and crazy designs on the faces... not to mention the crazy purple hair and the big red nose.

You'll Need:

- Paper Plate
- Markers
- Large Red Pom Pom
- Purple Yarn
- Scissors
- Glue

Directions:

1. On the back side of a paper plate, draw on eyes or use the general templates at the end of this section.

2. Color a clown's face, including the eyebrows, cheeks, and mouth.

3. Glue a large red pom pom onto the plate to make a nose.

4. Spread some glue around the outside of the paper plate and glue on purple yarn to make hair.

Simple Sun

Yes, this is a very simple project, but you can always make it more interesting for more capable children by gluing triangles around the outside of the plate to make the sun's rays, or even cutting around the outside of the plate to make the rays.

Most young kids will love this project because they get to paint.

You'll Need:

- Paper Plate
- Yellow Tempera Paint
- Paint Brush
- Black Marker

Directions:

1. Paint the back side of a paper plate yellow. Let dry.

2. Draw a face on the sun with a black marker.

Award

This is another really simple project, but kids will love making it for Dad. This project works especially well for Dad's birthday or for Father's Day.

You can also easily adapt this project to make awards for anything you would like to… For example: Best Teacher, Best Mom, Best Grandma, etc. You get the idea.

You'll Need:

- Blue Construction Paper
- Scissors
- Black Marker
- Glue Stick

Directions:

1. Cut two ribbon shapes out of blue construction paper. Make sure they are different lengths to make it look like ribbons instead of blocks of paper.

2. Glue the ribbon shapes to the front side of the paper plate so that they hang down.

3. Use markers to decorate the back side of the plate and make the an award for Dad.

Clock

This is another really simple project, but it can be used as a great teaching tool. One way to teach with it is to have the kids put the numbers on themselves, but another way to use it as a teaching tool is to make one and then use it in the classroom to teach time by moving the hands.

You'll Need:

- Paper Plate
- Black Construction Paper
- Markers
- A Brad
- Scissors

Directions:

1. Cut out 2 arrows from black construction paper to make the clock hands. Make one about 4 inches long and make one about 3 inches long. The clock's hands can be any shape you want.

2. With a bold marker, write all the numbers on the clock. Decorate the clock any way you want.

3. Push brad through the end of the 2 clock hands and through the middle of the paper plate. Spread the back of the brad out to secure it.

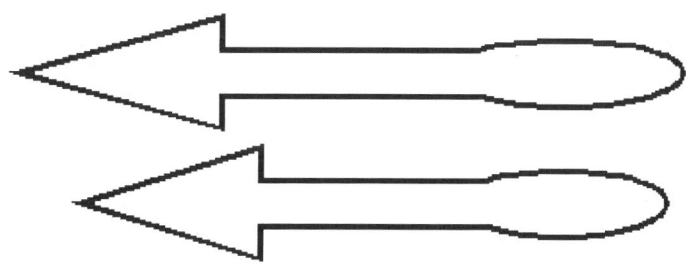

Winter Scene

I really like this project because it gives kids a really great opportunity to be creative while using something different than plain construction paper. I think it helps kids to see things a little differently.

You'll Need:

- Paper Plate
- Scrap Paper or Other Materials
- Scissors
- Markers
- Glue

Directions:

1. Use the front side of the paper plate as the basis for the scene.

Use any kind of scrap materials you want to create a winter scene, including paper, felt, ribbons, buttons, etc. along with markers.

You can also adapt this project to create other kinds of scenes. How about a spring scene with tissue paper blooms or a beach scene with real sand?

Picture Frame

I love it when you can make a craft with kids that's also somewhat useful. This picture frame is super easy for kids to make and they'll love it so much that you'll have to put it on the fridge or up in their room... especially if you use the child's picture!

You can also make these frames for gifts or as something to help your child remember a distant relative.

You'll Need:

- Paper Plate
- Tempera Paint
- Paint Brush
- Scissors
- Glue Stick
- A Photograph You Can Cut
- Frame Embellishments

Directions:

1. Paint either side of a paper plate any color you want. Let dry.

2. Cut a photograph into a circle that will fit inside the center of your paper plate.

3. Glue it to the paper plate.

4. Decorate or embellish your picture frame any way you want with ribbons, buttons, markers, glitter, etc.

Pizza

This project is a lot of fun to make! It's super simple and doesn't take a lot of materials, but the best part is that it actually looks like a pizza when it's done. Ooo… I'm hungry!

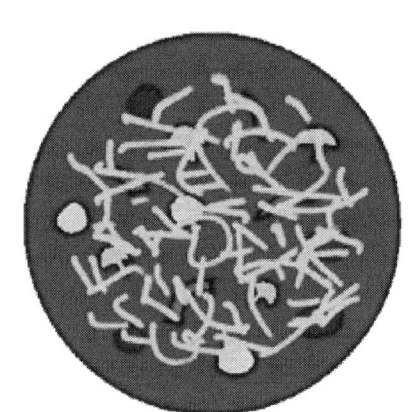

You'll Need:

- Paper Plate
- Scrap Construction Paper
- Red Tempera Paint
- Paint Brush
- Scissors
- Yellow or White Yarn Pieces
- Glue

Directions:

1. Paint the front side of a paper plate with red tempera paint. Let dry.

2. Cut pizza toppings out of construction paper… mushrooms, pepperoni, onions, peppers, etc. Glue them to the plate randomly.

3. Cut pieces of yarn into 1 - 2 inch pieces to make the cheese. Glue the yarn to the plate to complete the pizza.

Simple Ladybug

Ladybugs are always fun to make, especially in the spring when you start to see them hanging around! This is a very simple ladybug, but we also have a more complicated version later in the book.

You'll Need:

- Paper Plate
- Red Tempera Paint
- Paint Brush
- Scissors
- Black Marker
- 12 Inch Pipe Cleaner
- Hole Punch
- 2 Wiggle Eyes

Directions:

1. Paint the front side of a paper plate with red tempera paint. Let dry.

2. With black marker, draw head section, wing dividing line, and spots.

3. Use hole punch to make two holes about an inch apart on the outer edge of the head section. Thread a black pipe cleaner in to one hole, from the top down, then up through the other hole. Curl both ends around the marker to make the antennas.

4. Glue wiggle eyes onto the head section.

Wormy Apple

Your child will love this project! It's so much fun to do just about anything with a worm, and this one is so simple that you'll love it too!

You'll Need:

- Paper Plate
- Green Construction Paper
- Red Tempera Paint
- Paint Brush
- Scissors
- Black Marker
- Glue

Directions:

1. Paint front side of a paper plate with red tempera paint. Let dry.

2. Cut out a stem and leaf shape from green construction paper. Glue the leaf and stem to the top of the paper plate.

3. Draw a worm hole with black marker. Cut a worm shape from green construction paper. Glue the worm coming out of the hole.

Templates For Heads and Other Round Things...

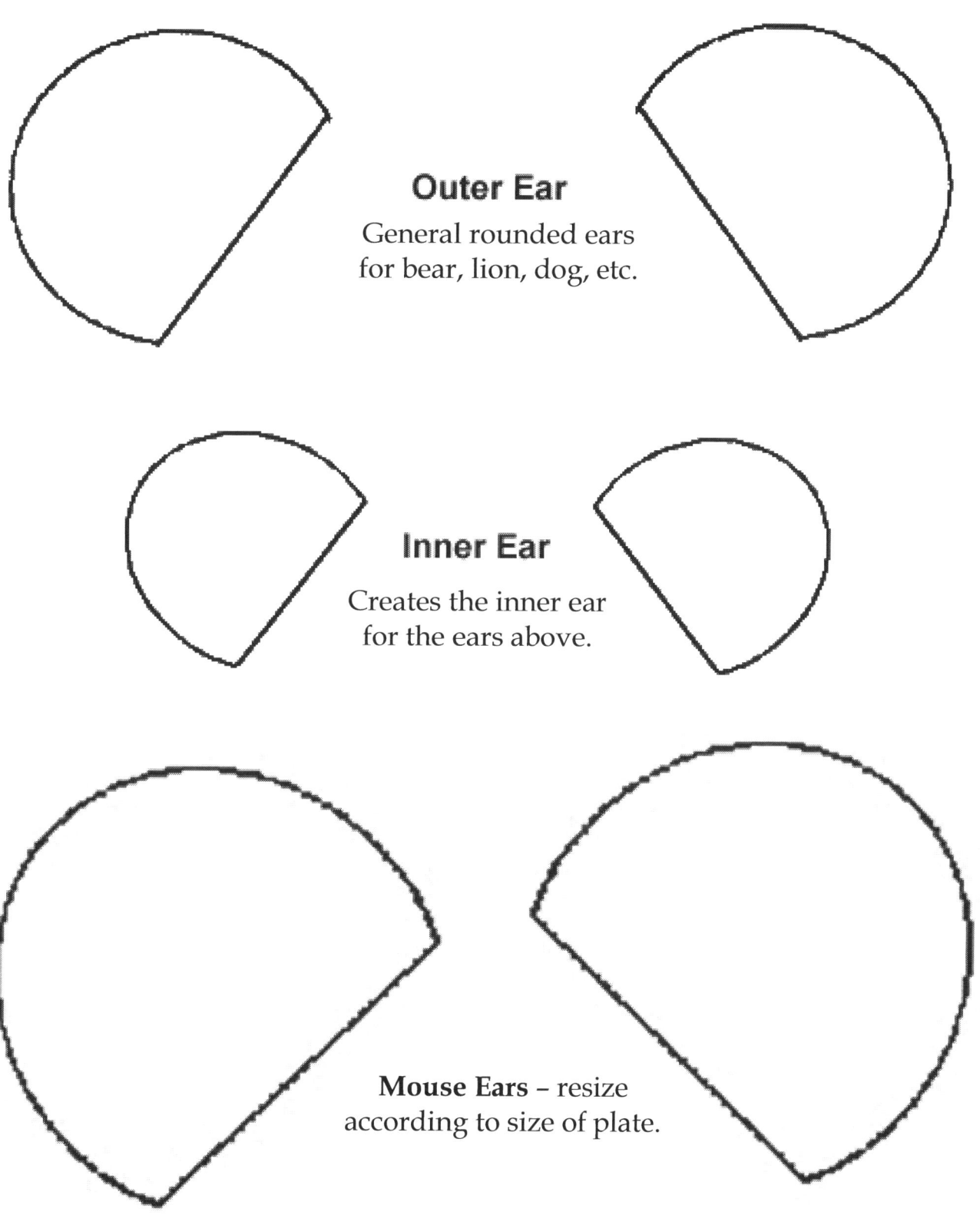

Outer Ear
General rounded ears for bear, lion, dog, etc.

Inner Ear
Creates the inner ear for the ears above.

Mouse Ears – resize according to size of plate.

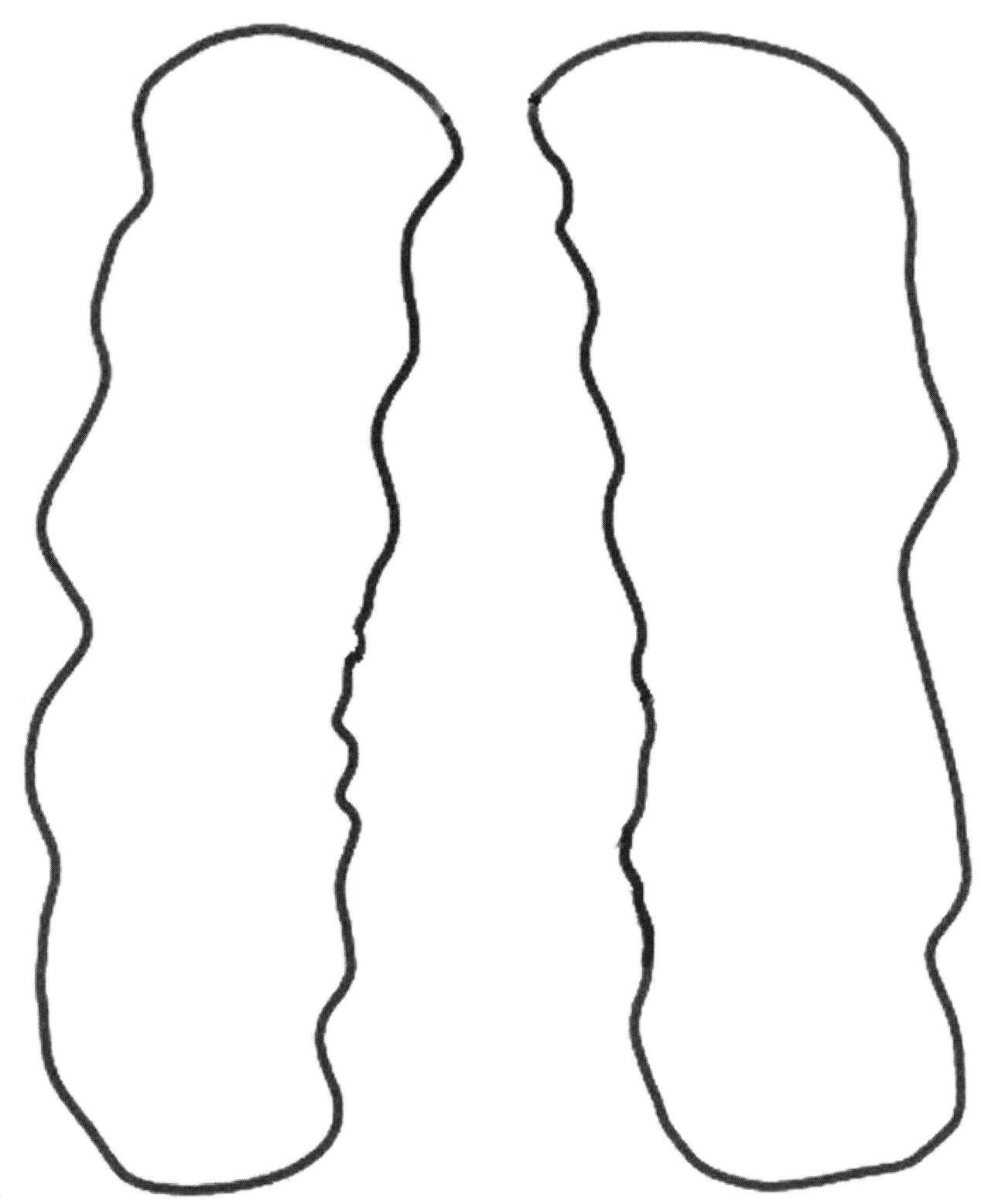

Floppy Dog Ears

Rabbit Ears

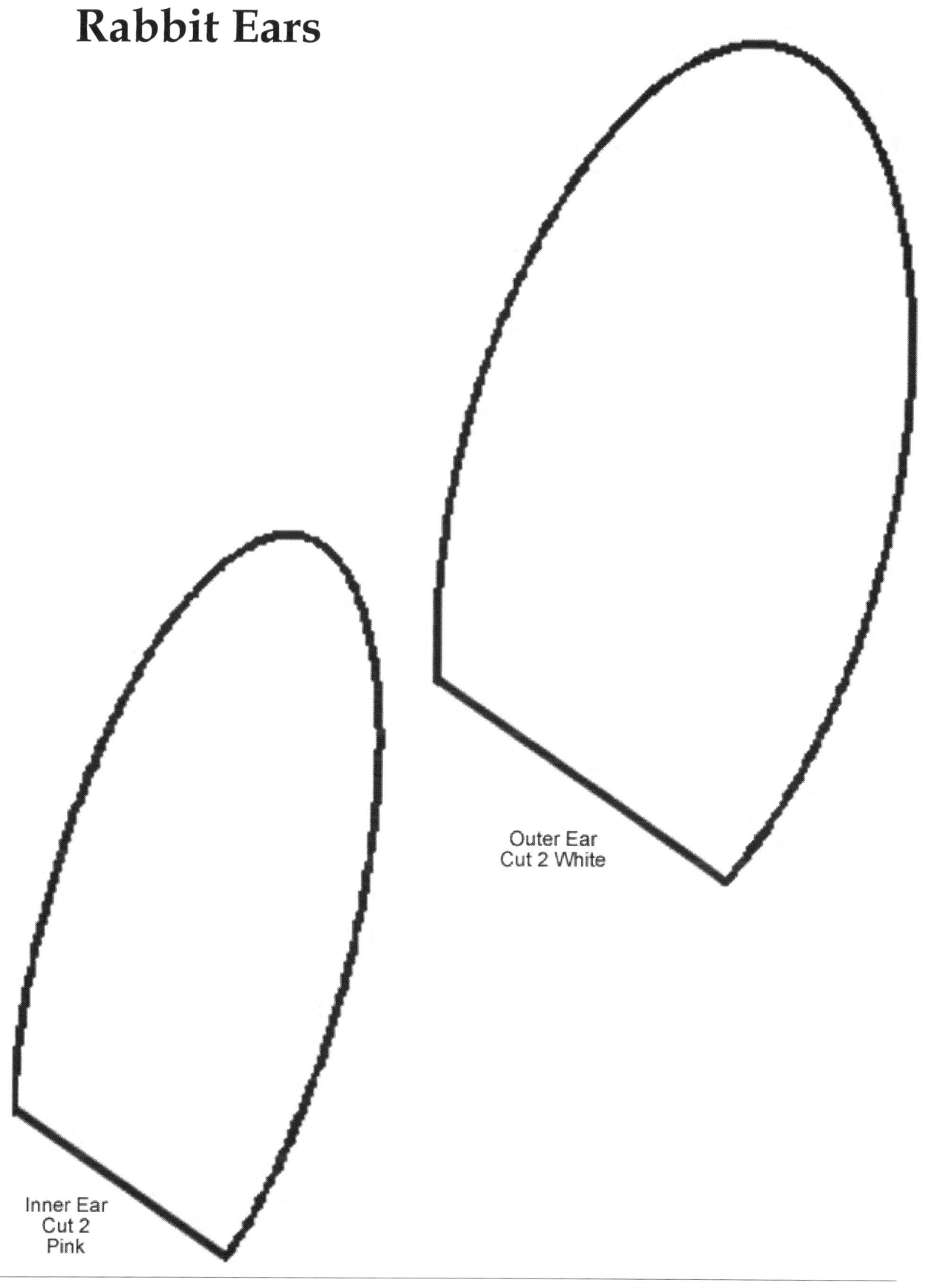

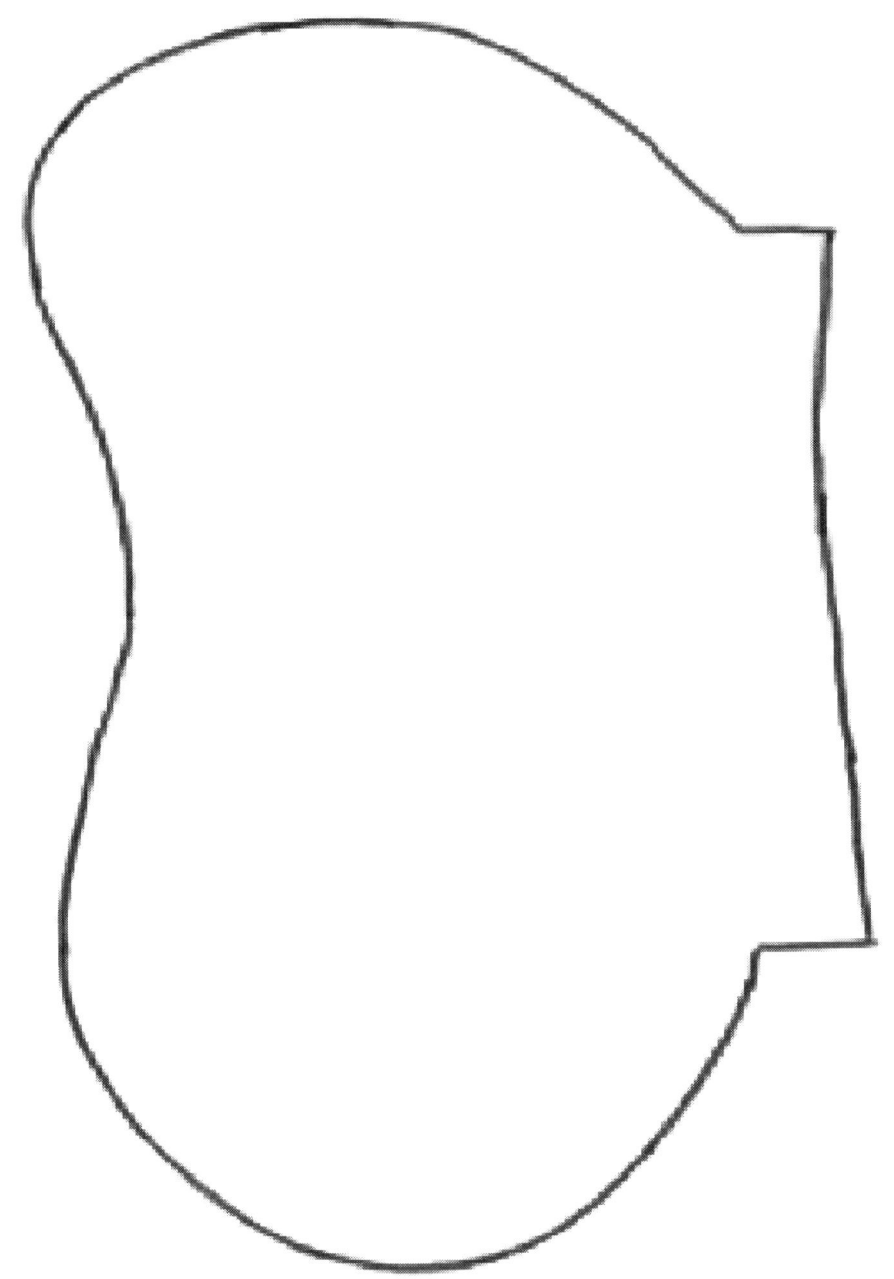

Elephant Ear (cut 2)

Elephant Template

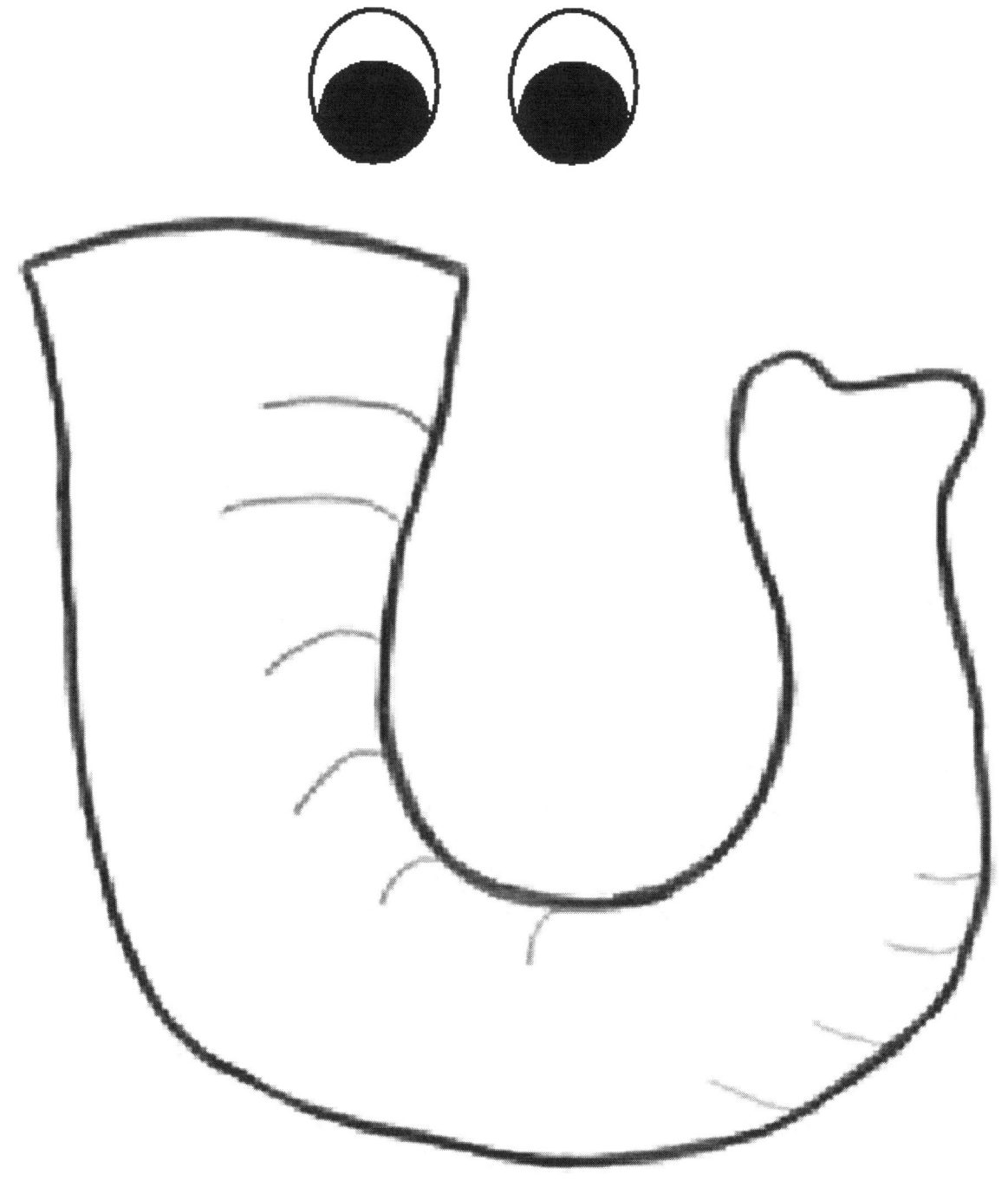

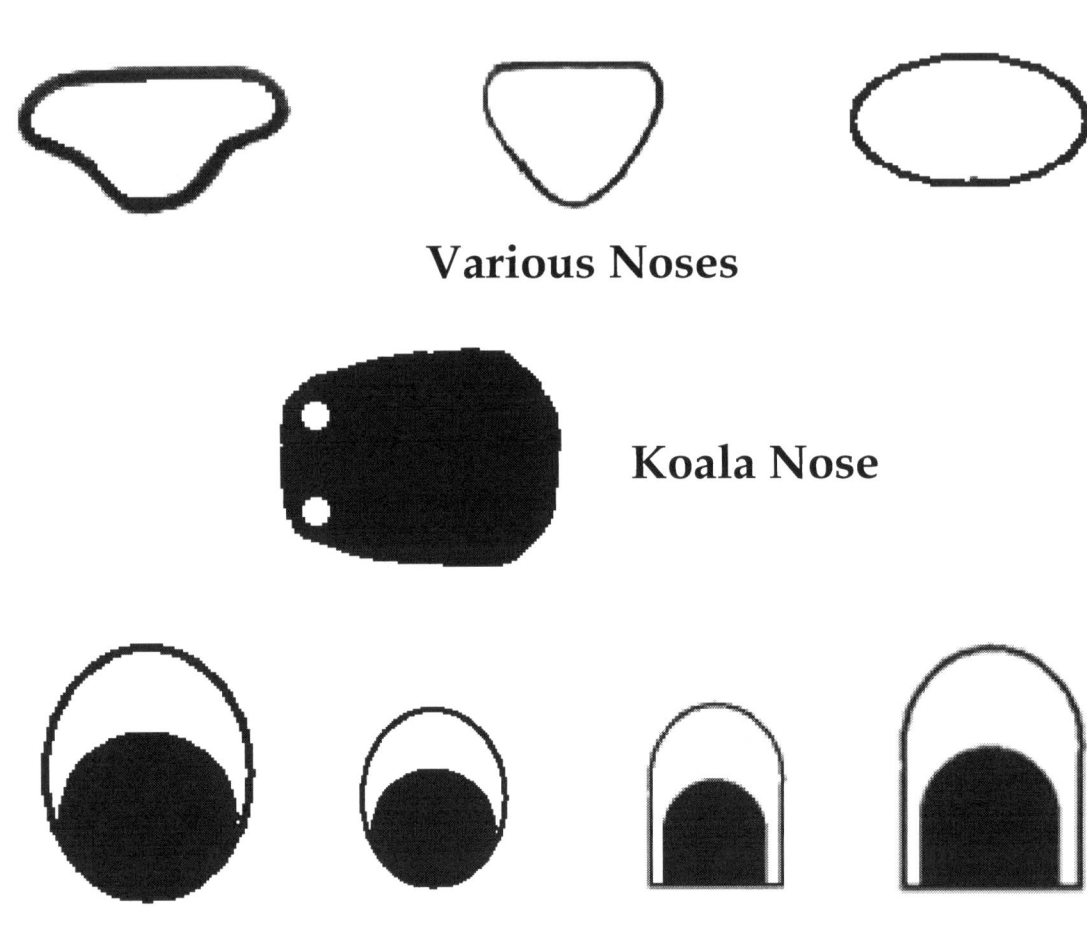

Various Noses

Koala Nose

Various Eyes

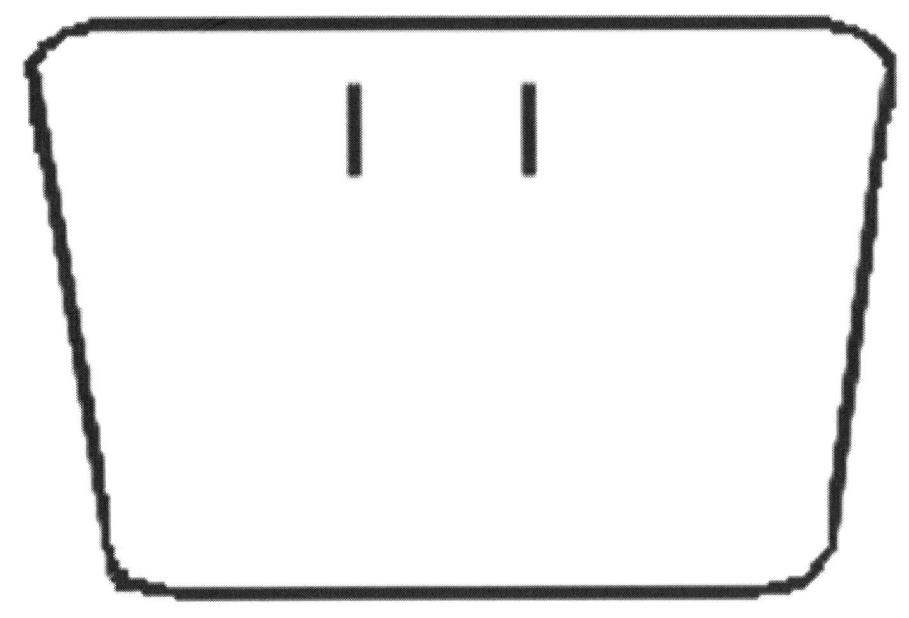

Duck Bill

Flat Animals...

The Low-Down on Flat Animals...

Creating flat animals out of paper plates is very similar to creating heads. The only difference is that the paper plate represents the body of the animal, instead of the head. Sometimes it even represents the body and the head. Many of the things we talked about in the last section also apply to flat animals, so I won't repeat all that in this section.

As you read this section of the book, keep in mind how you can change colors, features, add ons, etc. to get the most mileage out of flat animal paper plate crafts.

Creating Flat Animals

Creating flat animals out of paper plates is very easy. In general, all you have to do is paint the back side of a paper plate, let it dry, and glue on arms, legs, tails, etc. that you've cut out of construction paper.

The only thing you might find difficult about it is figuring out how to make the arms and legs - But I've taken care of that for you at the end of this section.

Let's move on to some flat animal projects...

Flat Cat

This is a really simple flat animal that can be adapted to be any kind of animal in the cat family... Tiger, panther, leopard, etc., or you could just make it your favorite family pet cat.

You'll Need:

- Paper Plate
- Gray and Pink Construction Paper
- Gray Tempera Paint
- Paint Brush
- Scissors
- Black Marker
- Glue

Directions:

1. Paint the back side of a paper plate with gray tempera paint. Let dry.

2. Cut out 4 skinny ovals for legs, 2 triangle ears, and a "J" shaped tail out of gray construction paper. You'll find templates for these parts in the template area at the end of this section.

3. Cut out a small triangle from pink construction paper for a nose.

4. Glue the legs and tail to the unpainted side of the plate so that they stick out.

5. Bend the bottom of each ear to make a slight tab. Glue the tab to the painted side of the plate so that the ears stick up from the flat cat.

5. Glue on the nose and draw on the rest of the face with a marker.

Flat Frog

As I mentioned earlier, I absolutely love frog craft projects. This one is so simple and fun, I'm sure your kids will love it too!

You'll Need:

- Paper Plate
- Green and White Construction Paper
- Green Tempera Paint
- Paint Brush
- Scissors
- Black Marker
- Glue

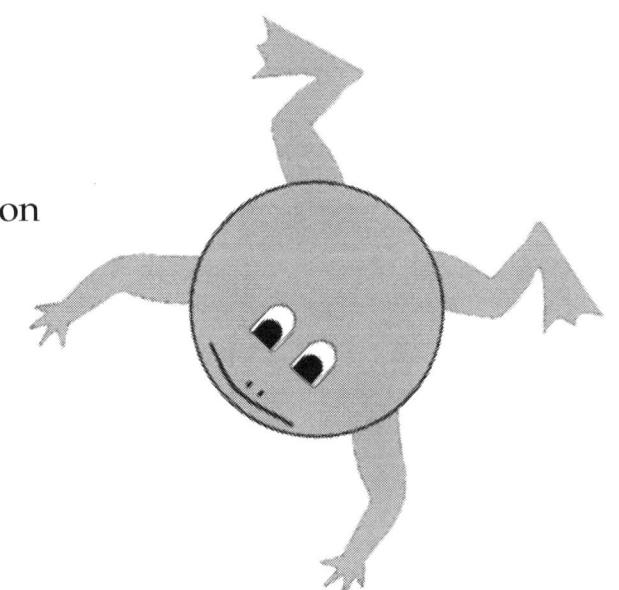

Directions:

1. Paint front side of a paper plate with green tempera paint. Let dry.

2. Cut 2 frog arms and 2 frog legs from green construction paper, using the template at the end of this section. Also cut 2 eyes from white construction paper.

Leave enough room at the bottom of each eye to make a tab to glue onto the frog.

3. Glue the arms and legs to the unpainted side of the paper plate. Glue the eyes to the painted side so that they stick up from the frog.

4. Draw on the frog's mouth with a black marker.

Turkey

Although it is traditional to make turkeys for Thanksgiving, you really can make them just about any time of the year. This one is a fun alternative to some of the traditional turkey crafts you may have seen.

You'll Need:

- Paper Plate
- Brown, Orange, Red, and Yellow Construction Paper
- Scissors
- Markers
- Glue

Directions:

1. Cut several long skinny tear drop shapes out of various colors of construction paper. They should be at least 10 inches long. These will be the turkey's feathers.

2. Cut out the turkey's head and body from yellow or brown construction paper.

> You can use the template for the head and body and the feathers in the templates area at the end of this section.

3. Glue the feathers onto the plate so that they fan out around the plate. They should cover the plate.

4. Glue the turkey's body on top of the feathers. Draw the eyes, waddle, and beak onto the turkey with markers.

Flat Duck

This is another one of the flat animals that I think is really fun… and kids will too! You could even dress this one up by gluing on a few feathers if you want.

You'll Need:

- Paper Plate
- Orange and Yellow Construction Paper
- Yellow Tempera Paint
- Paint Brush
- Scissors
- Black Marker
- Glue

Directions:

1. Paint back side of a paper plate with yellow tempera paint. Let dry.

2. Cut out the duck's bill and feet from orange construction paper. Cut out the wings from yellow construction paper. The templates are in the template area at the end of this section.

3. Glue the bill onto the edge of the painted side of the plate. Glue the wings to the painted side of the plate on either side of the bill. Glue the feet onto the unpainted side of the plate, opposite the side with the bill, so that they stick out from the plate.

4. Draw eyes on with a marker, or glue on the eyes you've cut out.

Turtle

Kids always enjoy making turtles, and this one is really easy and very cute when it's finished.

You'll Need:

- Paper Plate
- Green Construction Paper
- Green Tempera Paint
- Paint Brush
- Scissors
- Black Marker
- Glue

Directions:

1. Paint back side of a paper plate with green tempera paint. Let dry.

2. Cut the feet, tail, and head from green construction paper, using the templates at the end of this section.

The tail is just a triangle.

3. Glue the feet, tail, and head to the unpainted side of the paper plate so that they stick out from the plate.

4. Draw a face on the head with a black marker.

Flat Sheep

I think this craft project is really cute, but not because it's made out of a paper plate or because it's flat, but because it's covered in cotton balls. What a great way to give younger kids an additional sensory experience!

You'll Need

- Paper Plate
- White Construction Paper
- Cotton Balls
- Scissors
- Black and Pink Marker
- Glue

Directions

1. Cut 4 identical rectangles out of white construction paper. They should measure about 4 x 2 inches.

2. Cut out 2 ears from the template area at the end of this section, and 2 eyes and a nose using the templates at the end of the previous section. (Or you could just draw on all these parts with a black marker.)

2. Glue the rectangle feet to the front side of the paper plate (the side you would normally eat on). Glue the other parts to the back side of the paper plate (or draw them on).

3. Draw on the mouth and color the nose pink with markers.

4. Spread glue over the paper plate and cover with cotton balls.

Tropical Fish

You could probably make this fish look like any kind of fish you want, but I think it kind of looks like an angelfish.

You'll Need

- Paper Plate
- Blue Construction Paper
- Green Tempera Paint
- Paint Brush
- Scissors
- Black Marker
- Glue

Directions

1. Paint the back side of a paper plate with green tempera paint. Let dry.

2. Cut a large crescent of blue construction paper. It should be about 2 inches at it's widest point and about 12 inches long (you'll have to adjust if you're plate isn't a standard size).

3. Cut a second crescent that's about the same width and 6 - 8 inches long.

4. Glue the large crescent to the middle of the plate. Glue the small crescent to the edge of the plate to make the tail.

4. Draw on an eye and a mouth with the black marker.

Flat Cow

Kids will really like this craft because of the spots all over it. Of course you could make a different kind of cow, but it just wouldn't be as fun!

You'll Need:

- Paper Plate
- White Construction Paper
- Scissors
- Black and Pink Marker
- Yarn
- Glue

Directions:

1. Cut 4 identical rectangles out of white construction paper. They should measure about 4 x 2 inches.

2. Cut out 2 ears from the template area at the end of this section, and 2 eyes and a nose using the templates at the end of the previous section. (Or you could just draw on all these parts with a black marker.)

3. Glue the rectangle feet to the front side of the paper plate (the side you normally eat on). Glue the other parts to the back side of the paper plate (or draw them on).

4. Use a black marker to make spots all over the plate and the legs. Color the nose pink.

5. Glue a piece of yarn to the un-spotted side of the plate to make a tail.

Flat Leopard

Notice that the spots on this fun flat cat aren't just simple black spots. They're brown spots outlined with black.

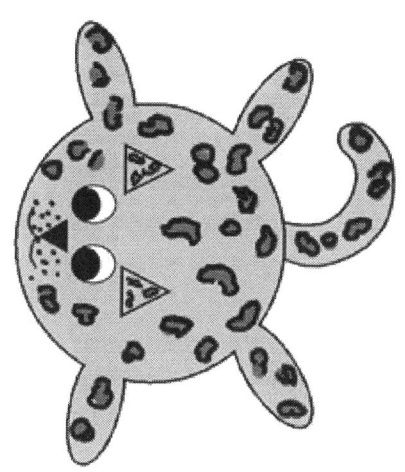

You'll Need:

- Paper Plate
- Light Brown or Yellow Construction Paper
- Light Brown or Yellow Tempera Paint
- Paint Brush
- Scissors
- Black and Brown Markers
- Glue

Directions:

1. Paint the back side of a paper plate with light brown or yellow tempera paint. Let dry.

2. Cut 4 skinny ovals for legs, 2 triangle ears, and a "J" shaped tail out of light brown or yellow construction paper. Cut out a small triangle from black construction paper for a nose.

3. Glue the legs and tail to the unpainted side of the plate so that they stick out.

4. Bend the bottom of each ear to make a slight tab. Glue the tab to the painted side of the plate so that the ears stick up from the leopard.

5. Glue on the nose and draw on the rest of the features with a marker.

6. Draw leopard spots all over the animal with brown and black markers.

Crab

I really like this paper plate craft because it's really simple, but also because it's an animal that you don't see kids making very often.

You'll Need:

- Paper Plate
- Red Construction Paper
- Red Tempera Paint
- Paint Brush
- Scissors
- Black Marker
- Glue

Directions:

1. Paint the back side of a paper plate with red tempera paint. Let dry.

2. Cut out 2 crab claws and 6 crab legs out of red construction paper, using the templates from the end of this section.

3. Glue all the crab parts to the unpainted side of the plate so that they stick out.

4. Draw on the face with markers or cut out the eyes and glue them on to the face.

You could also use the eye templates from an earlier template section instead of drawing them… Or you could use wiggle eyes.

Raccoon

This is another one of the more unusual animals you can make using a paper plate. I hope this will give you a little inspiration for other animals that you can make on your own!

You'll Need:

- Paper Plate
- Brown Construction Paper
- Brown Tempera Paint
- Paint Brush
- Scissors
- Black Marker
- Glue

Directions:

1. Paint the back side of a paper plate with brown tempera paint. Let dry.

2. Cut the tail and 4 legs and 2 ears out of brown construction paper, using the templates at the end of this section.

3. Glue the tail and legs onto the unpainted side of the paper plate so that they stick out. Bend the tab part of the ear and glue it to the painted side of the plate so that the ears stick up.

4. Using a black marker, draw the stripes on the tail, the black tips on the feet, the eye spots, and the rest of the facial features.

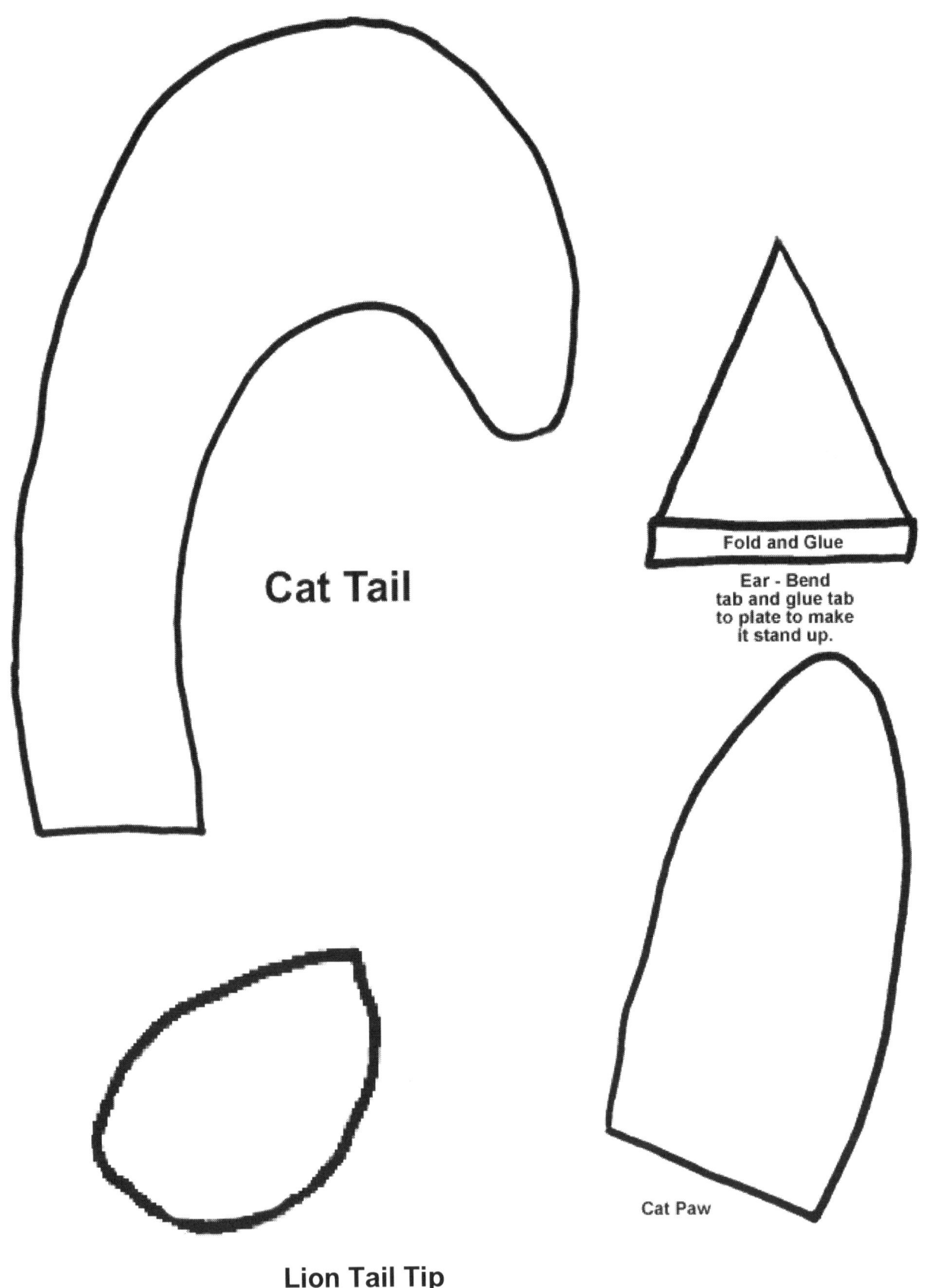

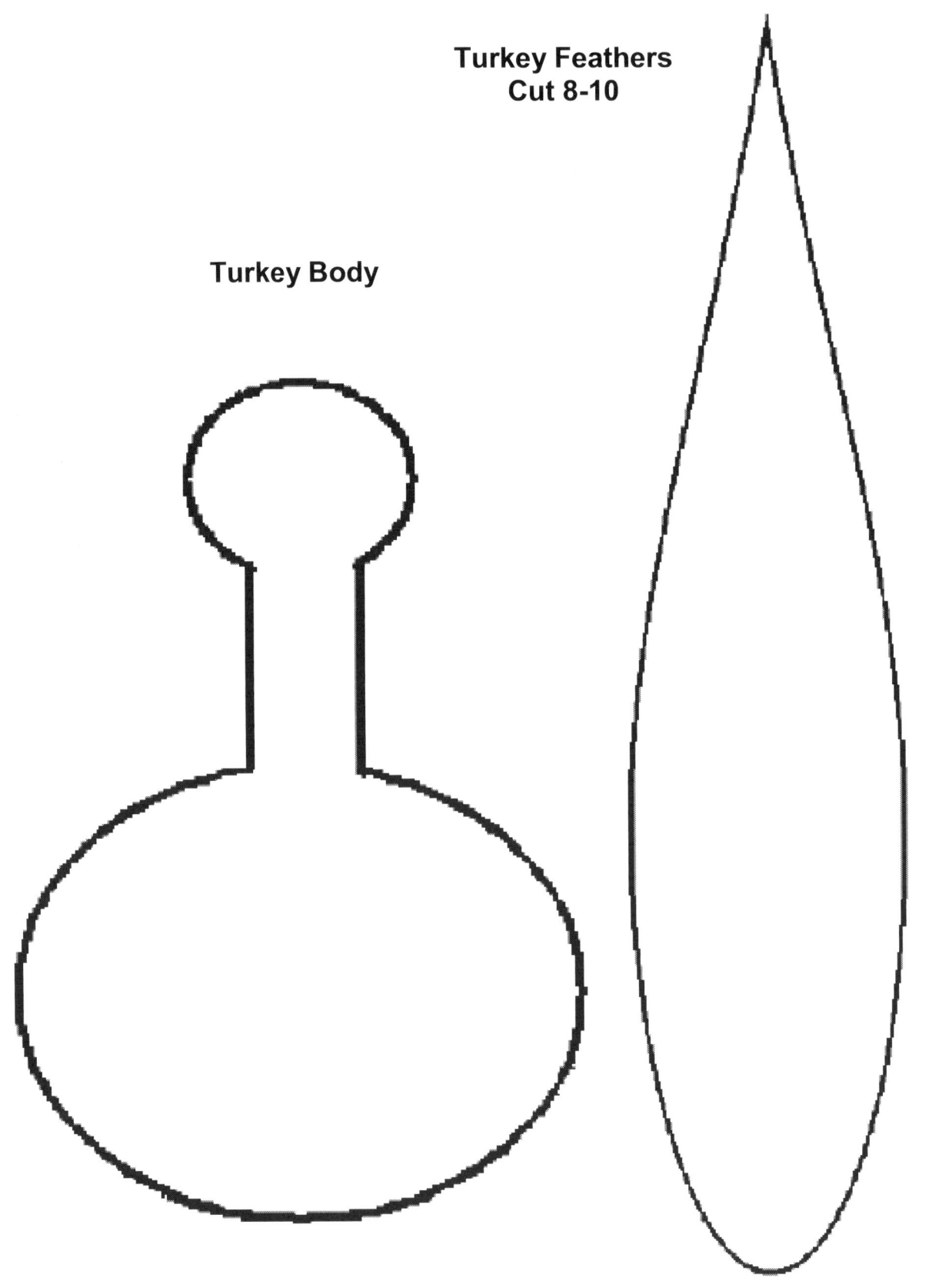

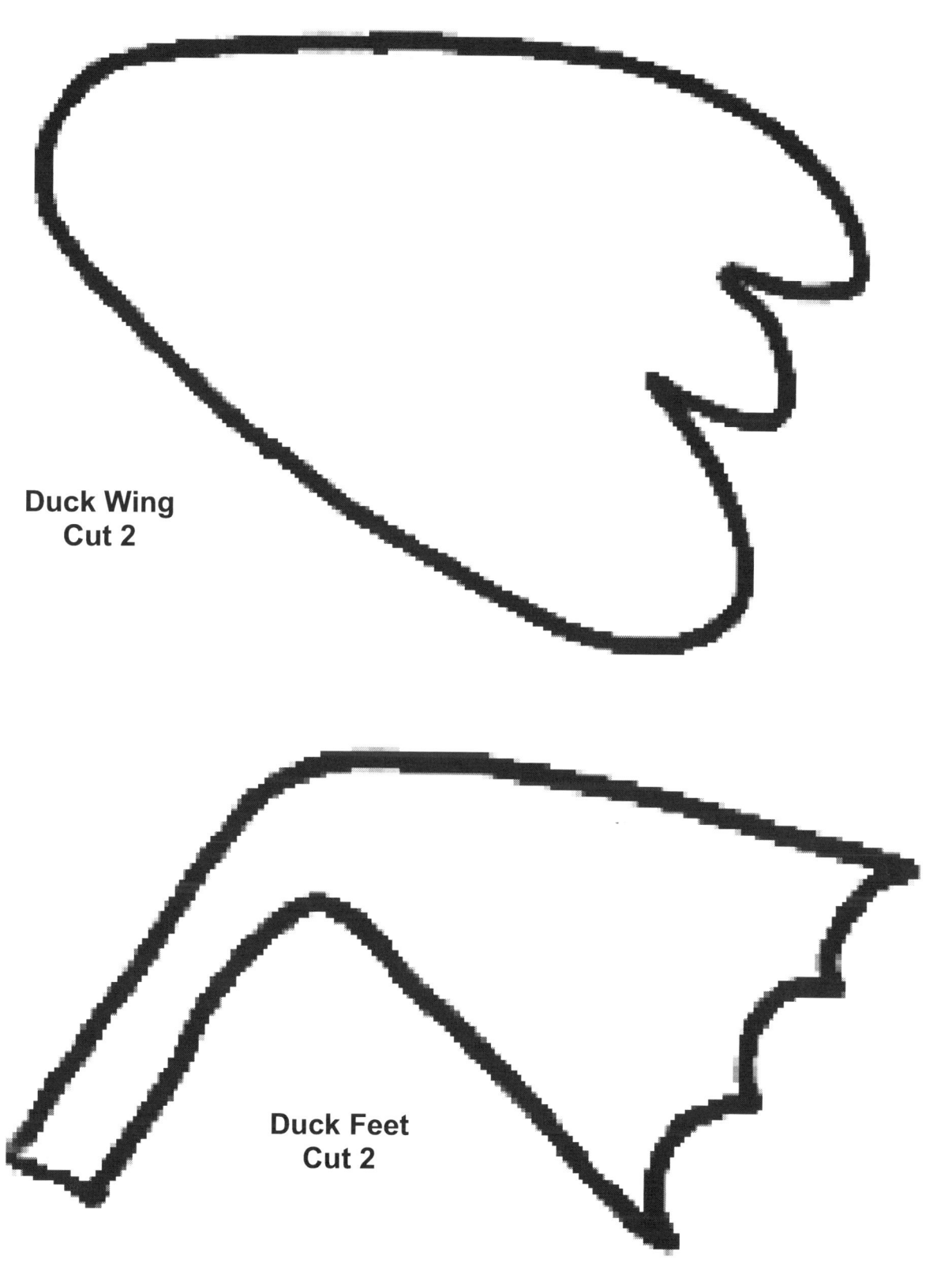

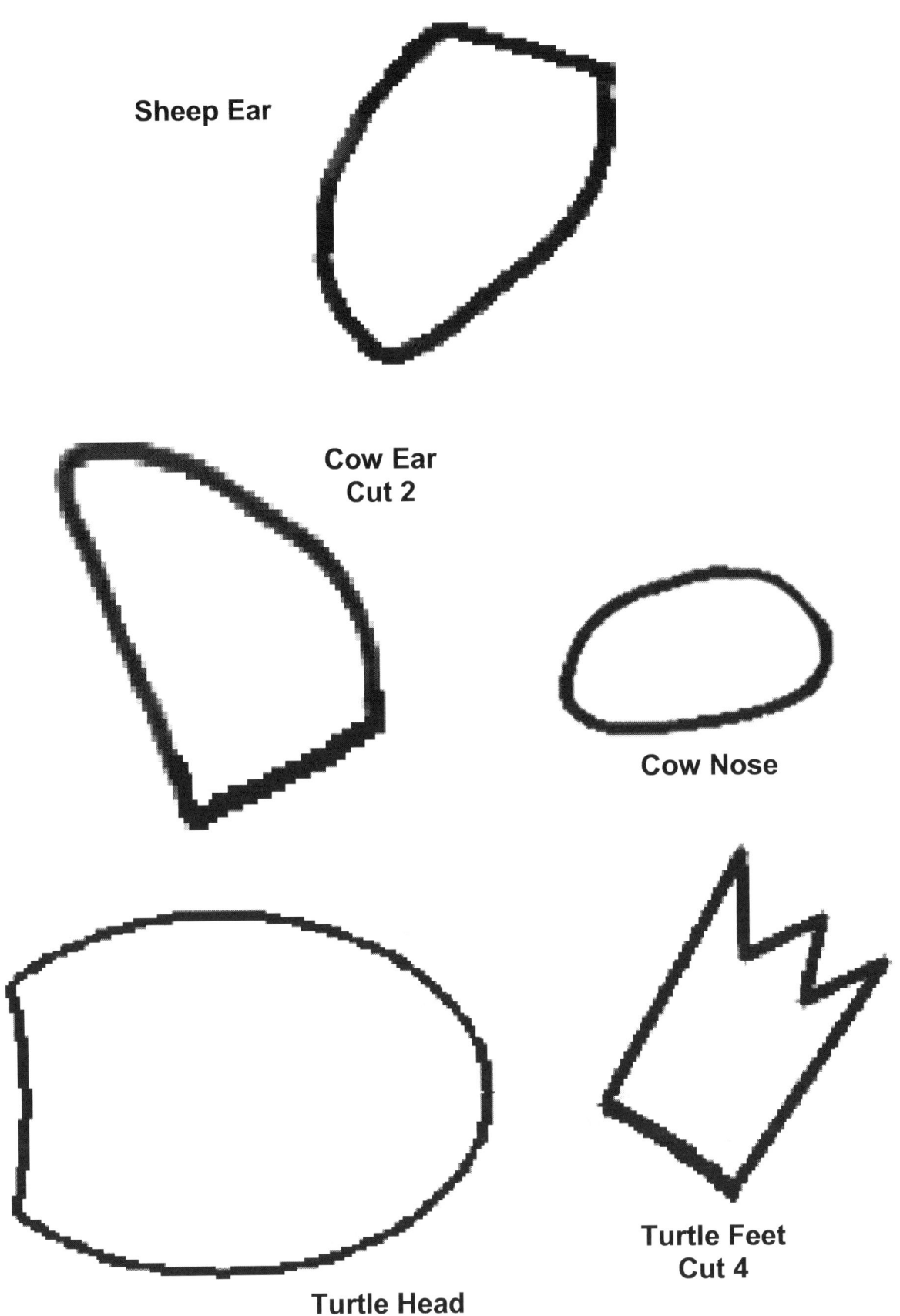

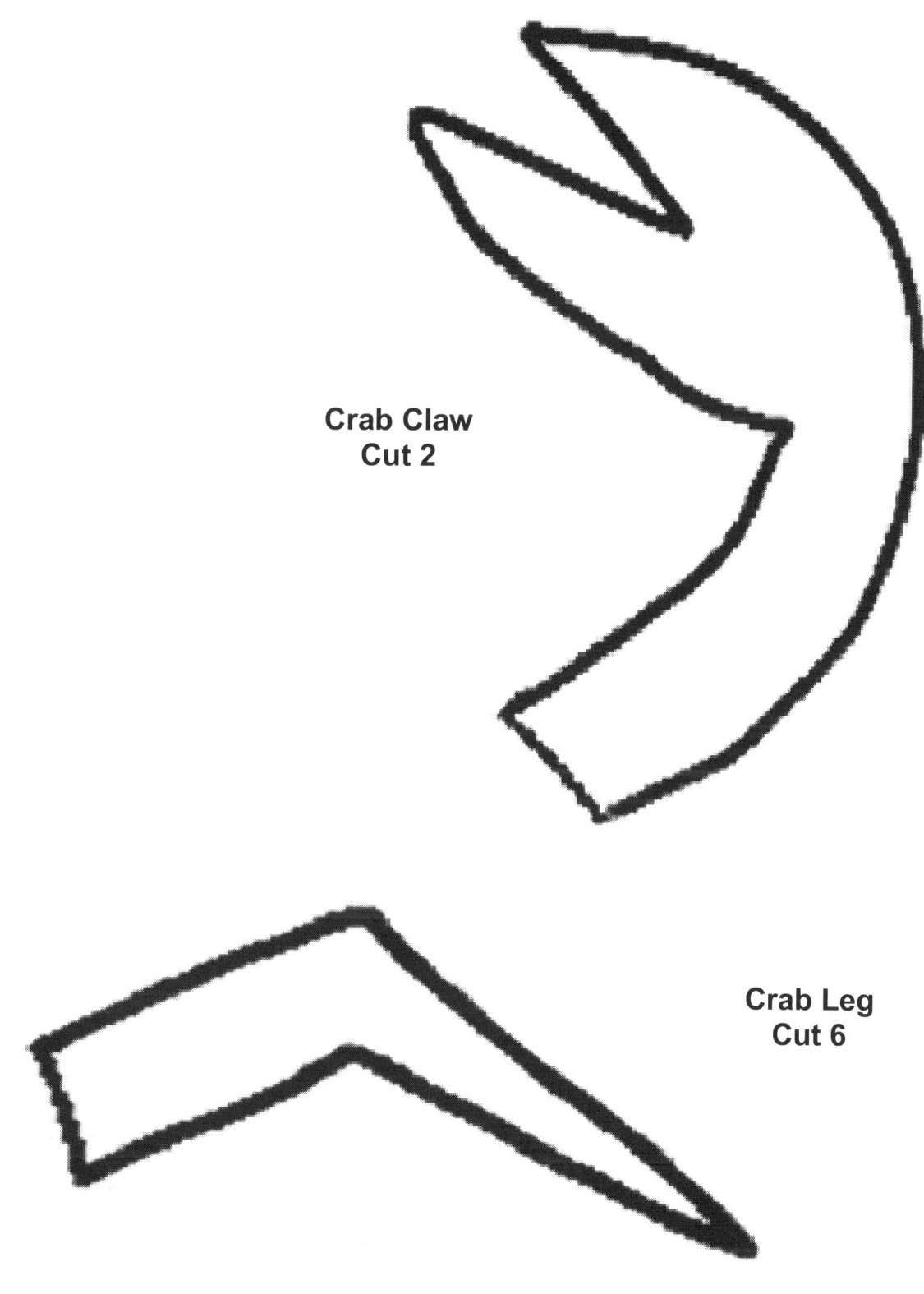

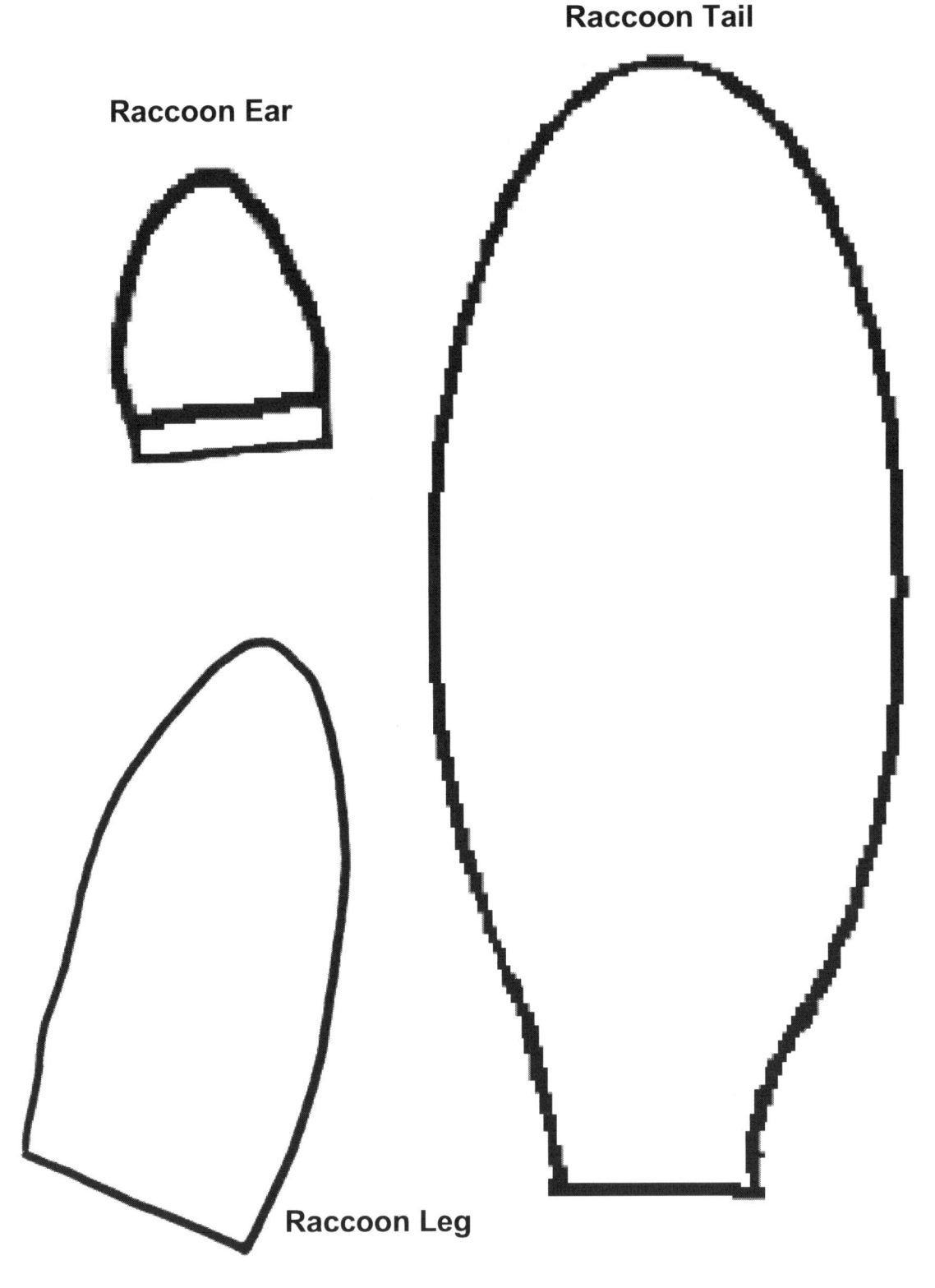

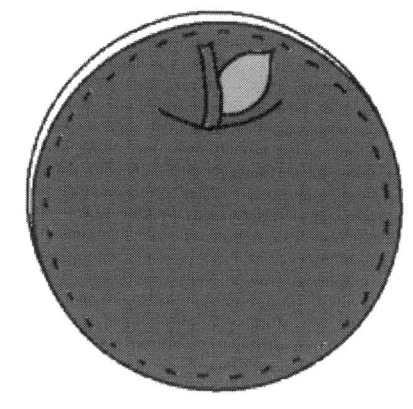

Multiple Plate Projects...

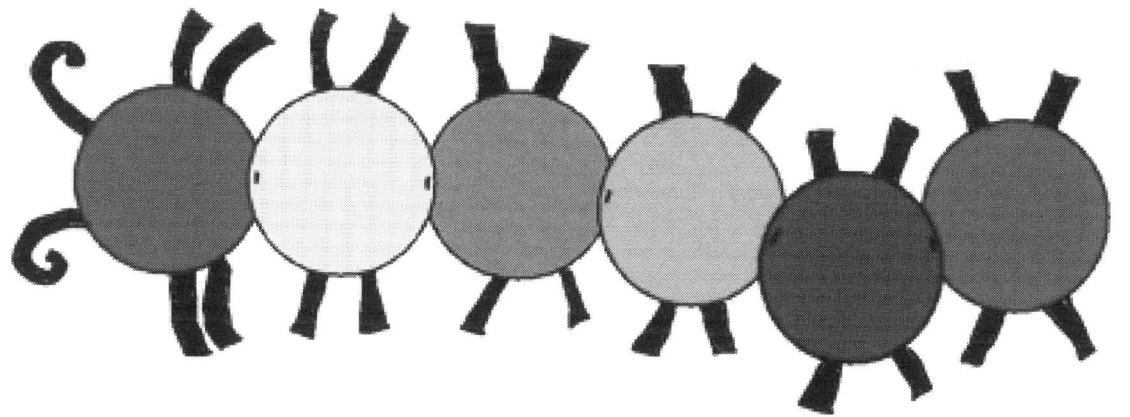

Now Things Are Getting Interesting...

Everything we've talked about up to this point has been extremely basic. Making paper plate animal heads and flat animals is super simple for even the very youngest children to accomplish. Now we're going to talk about the different kinds of projects that you can do using more than one paper plate.

Paper Plate Sandwiches

One of the key ways to use more than one paper plate is to sandwich other things between two paper plates and staple them together.

Here are a few examples of what I mean:

 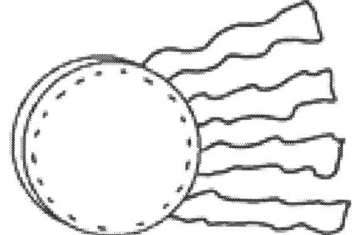

Other Round Parts...

Using multiple paper plates is also a good way to create objects and creatures that have multiple round parts. The best example of this is the snowman below:

You can use multiple paper plate projects as a creative way to make a wide variety of projects, especially when you remember the things we've already discussed.

Let's take a look at some project ideas...

Caterpillar

Although this project turns out really big, it's a ton of fun for kids to make! This would be ideal for a classroom of kids to make for a bulletin board or to put the name of the child spread out on the caterpillar's body.

You'll Need:

- Several Small Paper Plates
- Black Construction Paper
- Any Color Tempera Paint
- Paint Brush
- Scissors
- Stapler
- Marker
- Glue

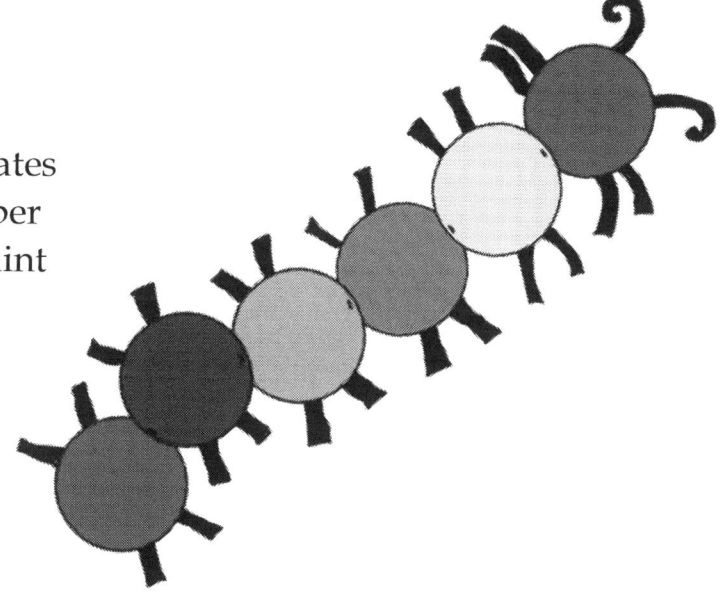

Directions:

1. Paint the back side of a small paper plate any color of tempera paint you desire. You will need one paper plate for each section of your caterpillar. Let paint dry.

2. Staple the paper plates together, edge to edge, until you have a chain of paper plates.

3. Cut 4 strips of black paper for each paper plate you are using. Glue each strip to the unpainted side of each paper plate so that it sticks out. These will be your caterpillar legs.

4. Glue 2 strips of black construction paper to the head of your caterpillar to make antenna. You can curl them around a pencil if you want. You can also draw a face on your caterpillar with a marker if you want.

Tired Lion

This is a clever way to make a lion that's very cute. I don't suggest attempting this project with very young children.

You'll Need:

- 1 - 9 Inch Paper Plate
- 1 Small Paper Plate
- Yellow Construction Paper
- Orange Construction Paper
- Yellow Tempera Paint
- Paint Brush
- Scissors
- Stapler
- Black Marker
- Glue

Directions:

1. Paint the back side of a large paper plate and the front and back of a small paper plate with yellow tempera paint. Let dry.

2. Using the templates below, cut 4 legs and tail out of yellow paper. Cut the lion tail tip out of orange paper. Cut 2 ears from yellow paper. Cut an orange mane that is slightly larger than the small paper plate that you're using.

3. Glue the orange tip onto the yellow tail. Glue the tail and legs to the unpainted side of the large paper plate. Glue the mane to the end opposite of the tail, on the painted side of the large plate. The center of the mane should be halfway between the two front legs and on the edge of the plate.

4. Fold the small paper plate in half, right sides together, and crease it. This is the head. Staple the head in the center of the mane. You just want to staple through the "lower jaw" so that the lion's mouth can still open.

5. Glue the ears to the head, near the fold. Draw the rest of the lion's features with markers. You can also draw in or glue in a tongue and teeth on the inside of the lion's mouth.

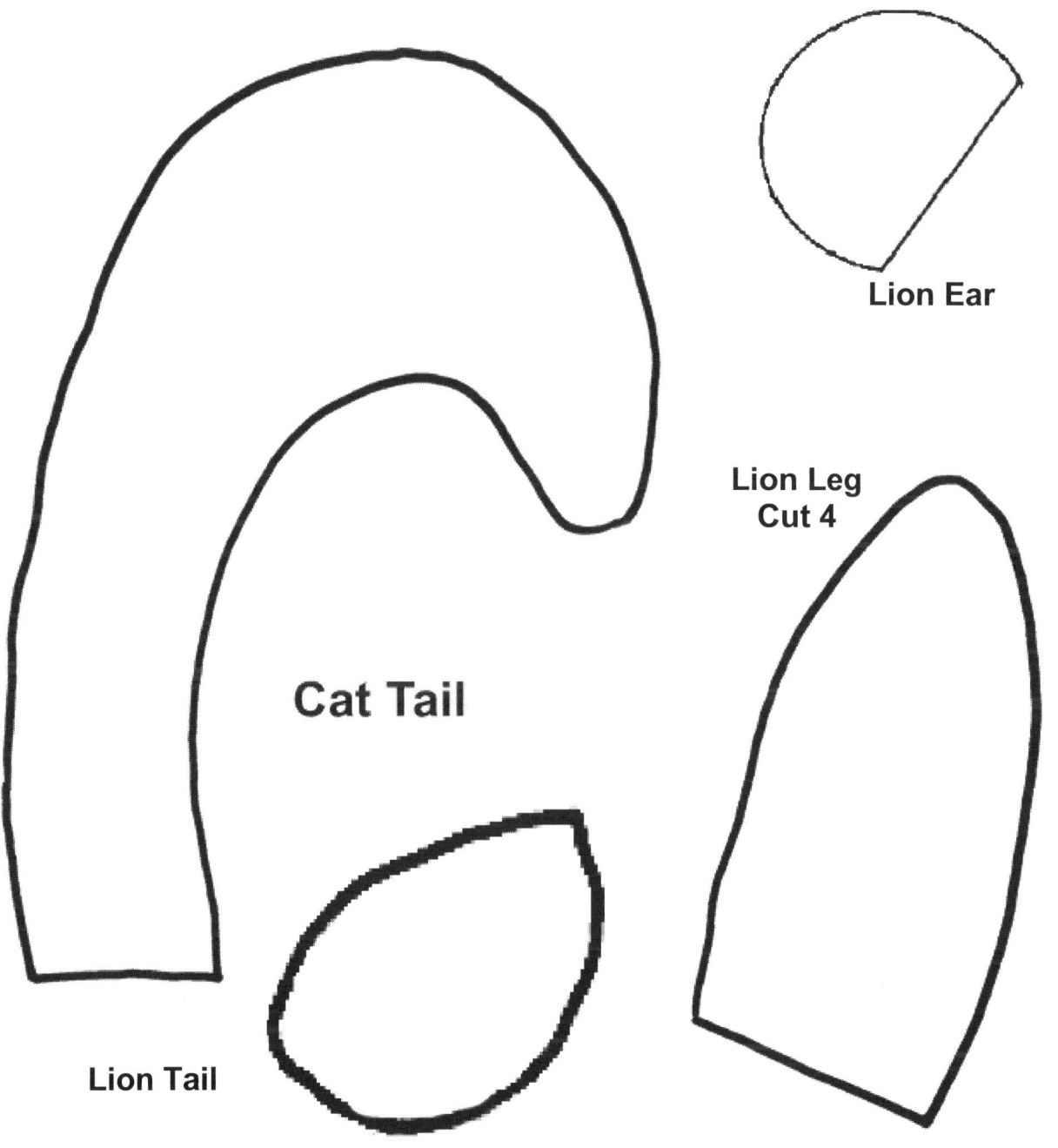

Funny Flat Frog

I absolutely love this version of the frog craft the best out of all the examples presented in this book. It's probably because of the tongue!

You'll Need:

- 1 - 9 Inch Paper Plate
- 1 Small Paper Plate
- Green Construction Paper
- Red Construction Paper
- Green Tempera Paint
- Paint Brush
- Scissors
- Stapler
- Black Marker
- Glue

Directions:

1. Paint the back side of a 9 inch paper plate and the front and back of a small paper plate with green tempera paint. Let dry.

2. Using the template on the next page, cut two frog legs and two frog arms from green construction paper. Also cut a long strip of red paper measuring about an inch wide and 8 - 10 inches long.

Using one of the general templates from the first section, print out 2 eyes.

3. Glue the frog's arms and legs to the unpainted side of the large paper plate.

5. Fold the small paper plate in half, right sides together, and crease it. This will be the frog's head. Staple the head halfway between the frog's arms, on the edge of the paper plate.

Make sure that you only staple through the bottom jaw of the head so that the frog's mouth will open.

6. Make a small tab on the bottom of each of your eyes and glue the tab to the back of the head near the fold. This should allow your eyes to stand up from the head a little.

7. Draw the nose holes on the frog's head with a black marker.

8. Curl one end of the red strip of paper around your black marker. Glue the uncurled end to the inside of the frog's mouth so that it looks like he's trying to catch a fly.

Funny Flat Frog

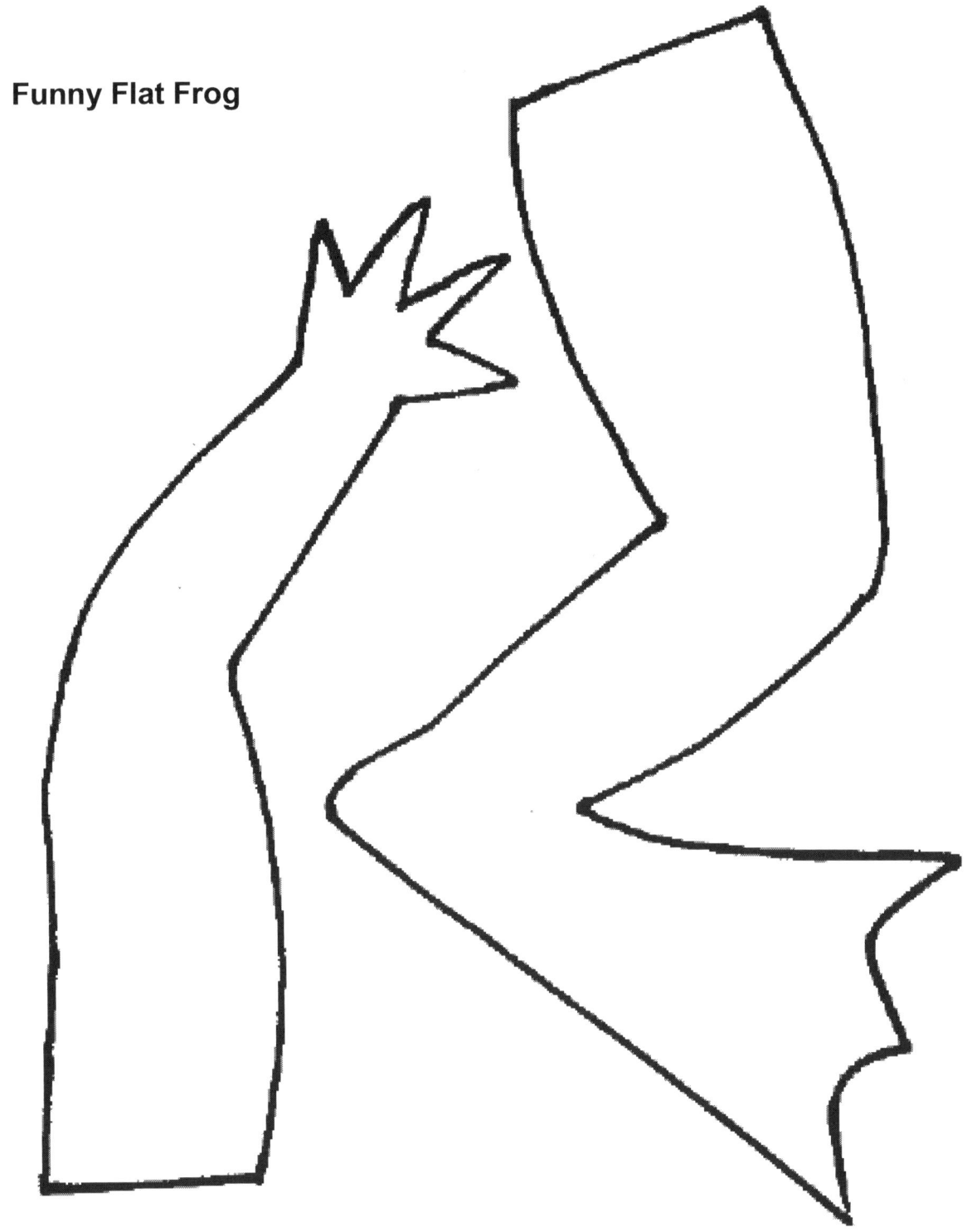

Apple Shaker

Kids will love making these little apple shakers... They love just about anything that makes noise!

You'll Need:

- 2 - 9 Inch Paper Plates
- Red Tempera Paint
- Paint Brush
- Stapler
- Markers
- Dried Pinto Beans

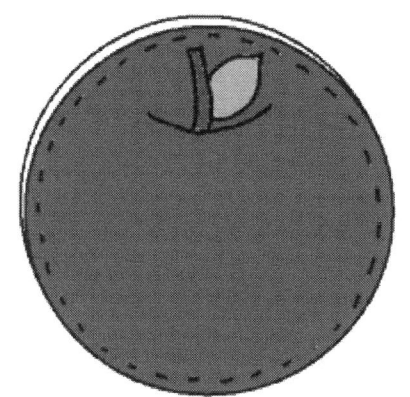

Directions:

1. Paint the back side of two paper plates with red tempera paint. Let dry.

2. Using a marker, draw in a stem and leaf for the apple. Use the picture below for placement.

3. Staple the two plates together, painted sides out, so that there is a space in between them. Staple closely together all the way around, but leave a hole at the top that's about 2 inches wide.

4. Slide a couple of tablespoons of dried pinto beans into the hole at the top. Staple closed.

Hand Puppet Puppy

Hand puppets are a lot of fun for kids of all ages, and this is a really quick and easy way to make one using paper plates. Although we've made a puppy here, you could easily make one using some of the examples in the first section of this book.

You'll Need:

- 2 - 9 Inch Paper Plates
- White Construction Paper
- Stapler
- Scissors
- Markers
- Glue

Directions:

1. Staple two large paper plates together, with right sides facing each other, to make a space in between them. Staple all the way around, but leave the bottom third of the plate open.

2. Cut out two ears, using the template on the next page. Glue them onto the paper plate.

3. Draw a face on your puppy with markers. Also draw spots all over face and ears.

4. To use it as a puppet, simply put your hand inside the dog's head, between the two paper plates.

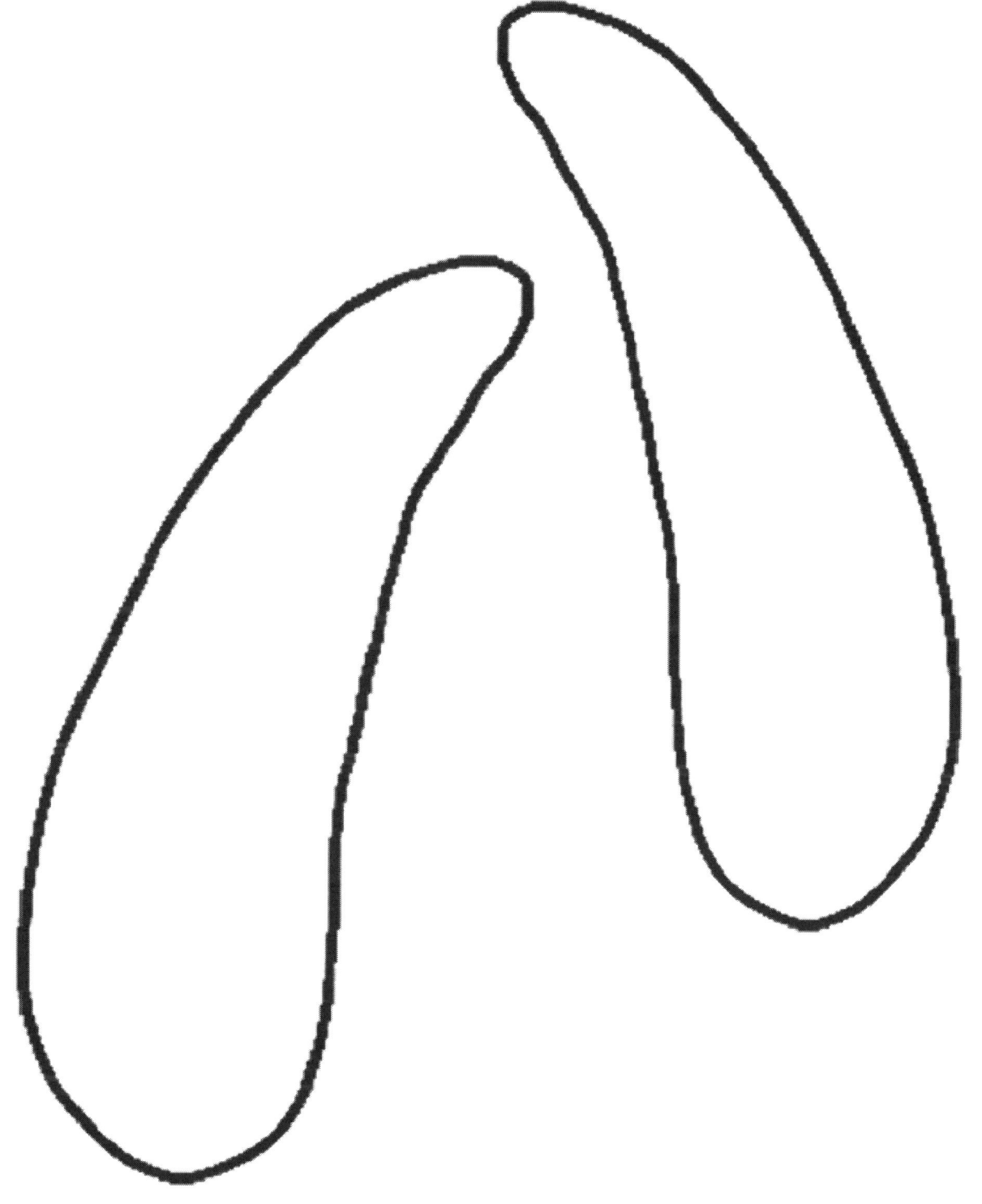

Silly Hat

This is a totally unique paper plate craft that I bet you've never seen before. It's super easy to make and looks really great when it's finished.

You'll Need:

- 2 Large Paper Plates
- Stapler
- Tempera Paint
- Paint Brush
- 24 Inches of Ribbon or Yarn
- Things to Decorate: yarn, ribbon, foam shapes, pom poms, paper, glitter, feathers, buttons, etc.
- Scissors
- Glue

Directions:

1. Paint the back side of one paper plate and the front and back side of the other with any color of tempera paint. Let dry.

2. Put the plates together with painted sides touching. Staple together in the center of the plates.

3. Cut 2 pieces of ribbon 12 inches long. Staple one piece of ribbon on either side of the plate that's only painted on one side. Staple the other piece of ribbon on the opposite side of the same plate.

4. From this point on, you can decorate the hat any way you want.

Quacking Duck

Unlike some of the other paper plate duck projects in this book, this one has a higher difficulty level and can easily be done with older kids.

You'll Need:

- 1 - 9 Inch Paper Plate
- 1 Small Paper Plate
- Yellow Construction Paper
- Orange Construction Paper
- Yellow and Orange Tempera Paint
- Paint Brush
- Scissors
- Stapler
- Black Marker
- Glue

Directions:

1. Paint the back side of a 9 inch paper plate and the front and back of a small paper plate with orange tempera paint. Let dry.

2. Using the template on the next page, cut two duck legs from orange construction paper. Also cut the 2 duck wings from yellow construction paper.

3. Using the template from the first section of this book, cut out 2 eyes for your duck if desired (or you can just draw them on with a marker when we get to that step).

4. Glue the duck's legs to the unpainted side of the large paper plate so they stick out. Glue his wings to the top of the plate.

5. Fold the small paper plate in half, right sides together. This will be the duck's bill. Staple the bill halfway between the duck's wings, on the edge of the paper plate. Make sure that you only staple through the bottom jaw so that the duck will be able to open his bill.

6. If you glue your duck's eyes on, make a small tab on the bottom of each of your eyes and glue the tab to the large paper plate near the bill. This should allow your eyes to stand up from the head a little. Draw the nose holes on the duck's bill with a black marker.

Folding, Bending, & Cutting...

Now For The Fun Stuff...

This section is where we get to some of the most creative projects that I've ever seen. There is no way that I can tell you every different way that you can cut, fold, or bend a paper plate to develop your own projects. What I can do is show you some basic techniques that you can combine with the techniques that we have already discussed. Put all these techniques together, and they'll be no end to what you can create.

Folding Plates

Here's a couple of ways to fold plates that you'll use a lot in your projects: fold the plate like a cone or fold it in half. Below are examples of each.

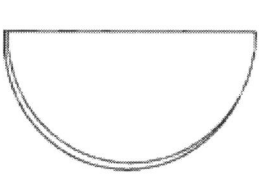 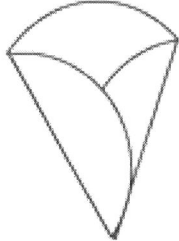

Halvsies

One of the great things about paper plates is that when you cut them in half you get a half circle. That may sound kind of dumb, but think of all the things you can do with a half circle.

 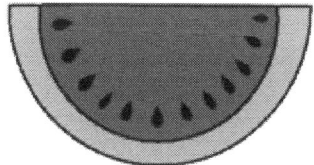

Other Cutting

There are probably about a million ways that you can cut a paper plate to use it for crafting.

You can cut around the outside of the plate to change the shape from round to another shape.

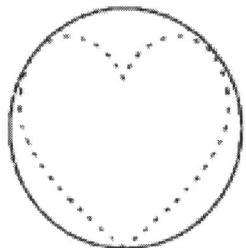

You can cut triangles around the outside edge to make the sun's rays.

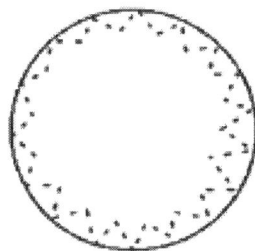

You can cut around the outside to make a flower.

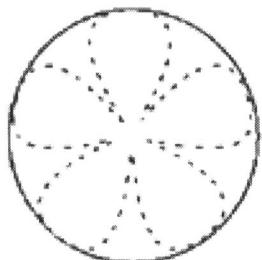

You can cut out the center to make a wreath.

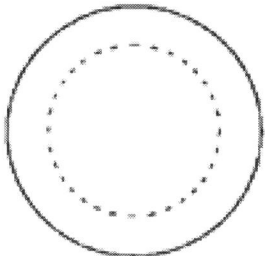

You can cut half the center to make a basket.

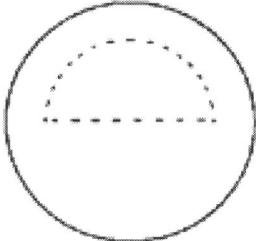

You can cut out eyes to make a mask.

You can cut it up into pieces and reassemble it into something else.

I'm sure you get the idea here. There are a lot of different ways to cut a paper plate.

Let's look at some projects so you can see what you can do...

Fall Wreath

We make paper plate wreaths using this same basic project each year for the fall. Sometimes we put fake leaves on for more color, but we usually just scavenge pretty leaves outside, making this a really inexpensive craft... Plus it's so simple that even the youngest kids can make one!

You'll Need:

- Large Paper Plate
- Fall Leaves
- Glue

Directions:

1. Collect a bunch of fall leaves.

2. Cut the center out of a large paper plate, leaving a ring.

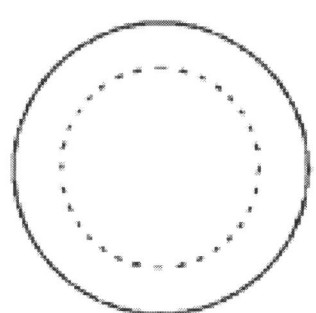

3. Spread glue onto the ring and glue your leaves to the ring.

If you try using fake leaves for this project, be sure to remove all the plastic "veins" so that they can easily be glued down.

Christmas Bow Basket

Everybody loves bows, and kids are no exception. This is a really easy project and makes a great Christmas decoration.

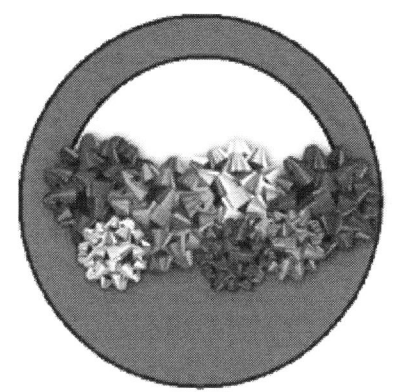

You'll Need:

- 9 Inch Paper Plate
- Green Tempera Paint
- Paint Brush
- Scissors
- Christmas Bows

Directions:

1. Cut a half circle out of the center of the paper plate to make a basket shape.

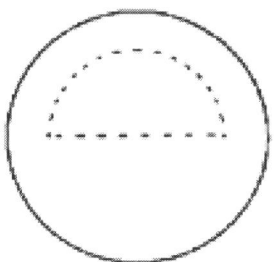

2. Paint the basket with green tempera paint. Let dry.

3. Stick Christmas bows around the top of the basket. You may have to tape or glue them instead of using the sticky stuff on the back of the bows to get them to stick.

Purple Brontosaurus

This is another one of those projects that's pretty easy to make, but I like it because it's kind of an unexpected way to use a paper plate.

You'll Need:

- 9 Inch Paper Plate
- Purple Tempera Paint
- Purple Construction Paper
- Scissors
- Paint Brush
- Stapler
- Black Marker

Directions:

1. Paint the back side of a paper plate with purple tempera paint. Let dry.

2. Using the template on the next page, cut 4 legs, a tail, and a head out of purple construction paper.

3. Fold the paper plate in half and staple once at the top. Slide the head in one side of the plate at the fold and staple in place. Do the same with the tail at the opposite end.

4. Glue the legs onto both sides of the plate, near the fold. Draw on face with a marker.

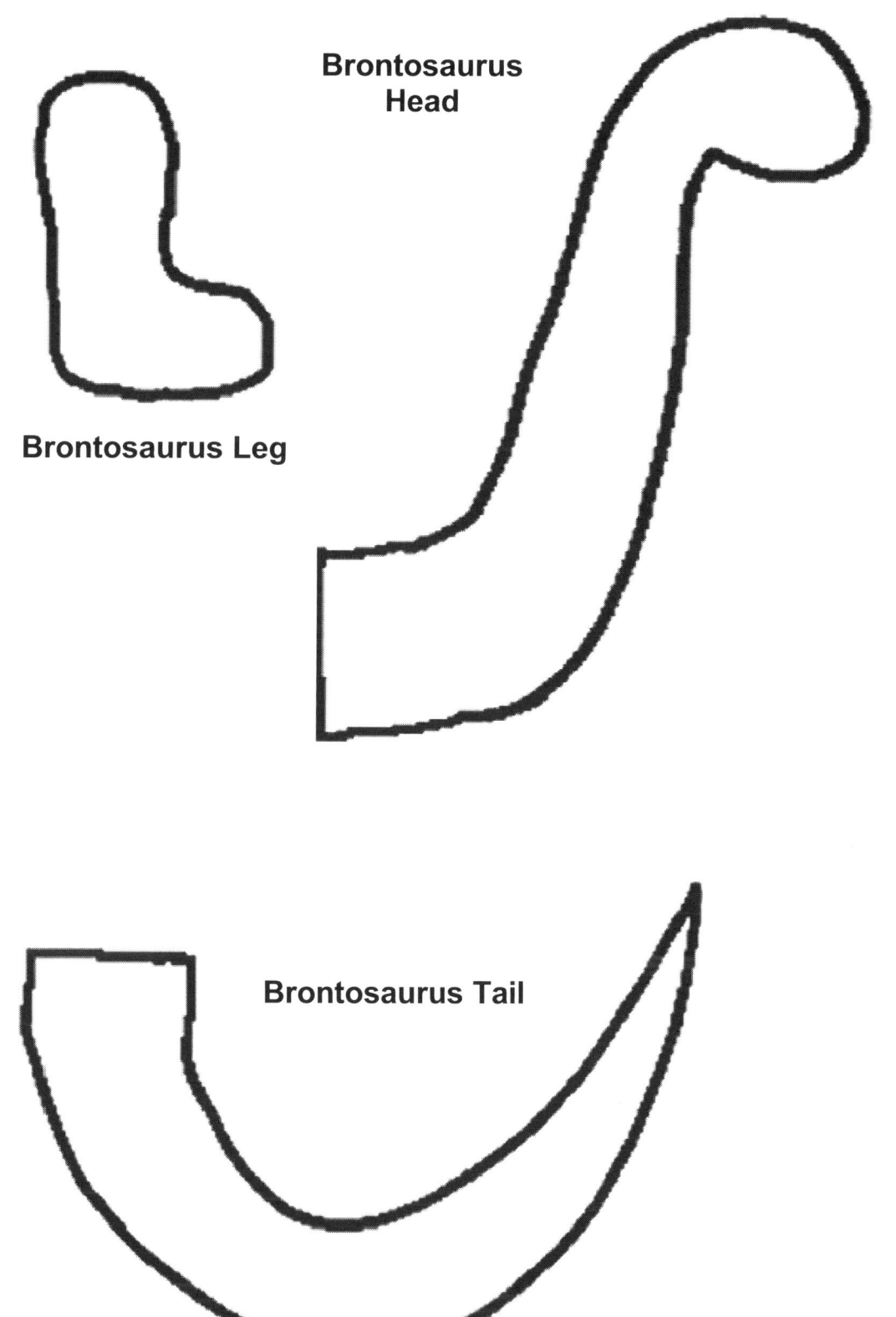

Sun Baby

This project is very similar to the picture frame craft that we did earlier in the book, but this one is a little more difficult to make because of the cutting. You may not want to do this with very young kids.

You'll Need:

- 9 Inch Paper Plate
- Yellow Tempera Paint
- Baby Picture
- Paint Brush
- Scissors
- Glue

Directions:

1. Paint the back side of a paper plate with yellow tempera paint. Let dry.

2. Cut small triangles from around the plate to make it look like the sun's rays.

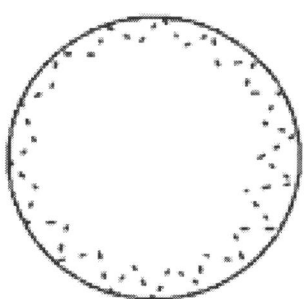

3. Cut the baby picture into a circle that will fit inside the sun. Glue in place.

Owl

This is a great project for kids who are a little bit older, but even some younger kids might be able to do it with a little help. They'll be so pleased with themselves when they see how the wings move!

You'll Need:

- 9 Inch Paper Plate
- Brown Tempera Paint
- Paint Brush
- 2 Brads
- Scissors
- Scrap Construction Paper

Directions:

1. Paint both sides of a paper plate with brown tempera paint. Let dry.

2. Use the template below as a guide to cut the plate as shown.

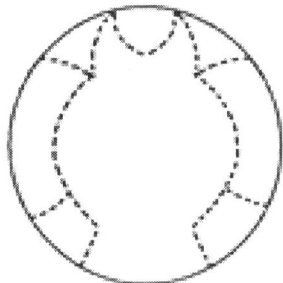

3. Use brads to attach the wings at the shoulders.

4. Use scraps of paper to make the eyes, beak, and feet.

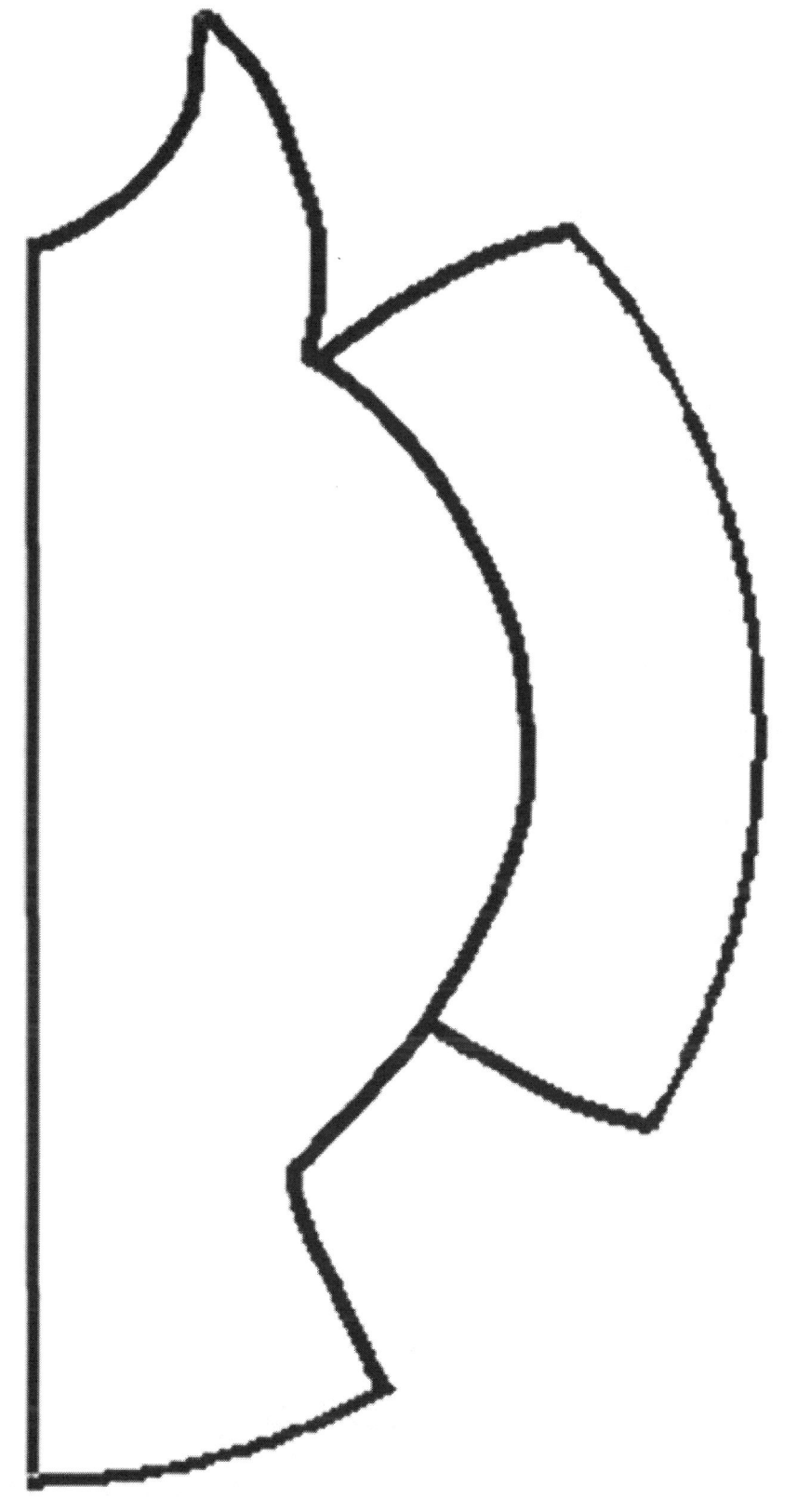

Stegosaurus

Stegosaurus is my favorite dinosaur, so I couldn't resist including him among the paper plate animals. Although a little more challenging, the templates should make it very do-able.

You'll Need:

- 9 Inch Paper Plate
- Green Tempera Paint
- Green Construction Paper
- Scissors
- Paint Brush
- Stapler
- Black Marker

Directions:

1. Paint the back side of a paper plate with green tempera paint. Let dry.

2. Using the template on the next page, cut 4 legs, head, and tail out of green construction paper. Cut several triangles from green construction paper as well.

3. Fold the paper plate in half and staple once at the top. Slide the head in one side of the plate at the fold and staple in place. Do the same with the tail at the opposite end.

4. Glue the legs onto both sides of the plate, near the fold. Glue the triangles onto both sides of the plate around the curved top. (Stegosaurus has two rows of plates.)

5. Draw on the face with a marker.

Stegosaurus Head

Stegosaurus Tail

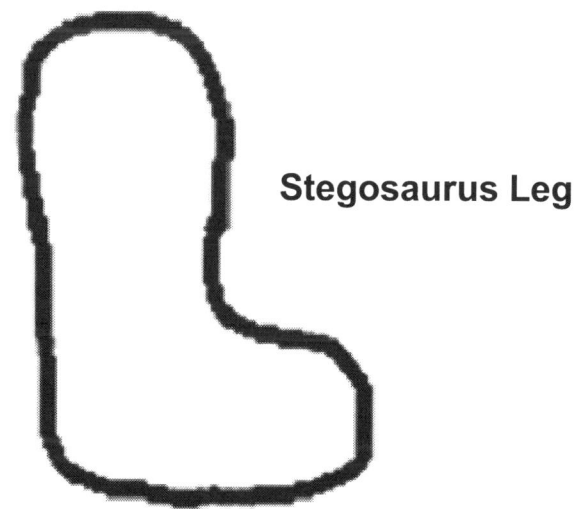

Stegosaurus Leg

Shapes Mobile

This is a great project if your child is just learning the names of the shapes. You might need to help them put the mobile together, but they'll get lots of practice with the shapes.

You'll Need:

- 1 Paper Plate
- Construction Paper
- Scissors
- Hole Punch
- Yarn

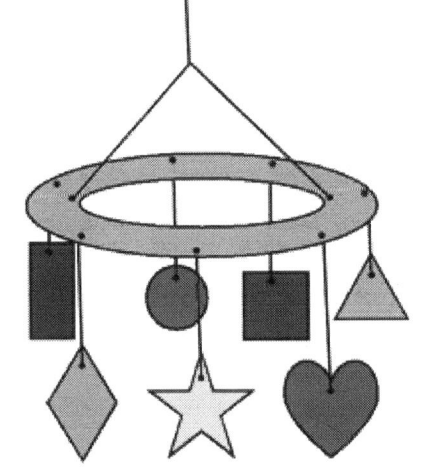

Directions:

1. Cut the center out of a paper plate, making a ring. Paint if desired, or leave white.

2. Cut several different shapes out of different colors of construction paper. (This is a good opportunity for children to practice naming colors and shapes.)

3. Punch as many holes as you have shapes around the outside edge of your paper plate ring. Try to space the holes evenly. Punch a hole in the top of each construction paper shape. Also two holes on opposite sides of the inside of the ring.

4. Tie a piece of yarn through the hole in each shape and then tie the other end through a hole in your plate ring. Do this with all the shapes. Thread a piece of yarn through the two holes on the inside of the ring and then tie the ends together to make a hanger for your mobile.

Spiral Easter Egg Mobile

This project shows you another great way to make a mobile out of a paper plate. Younger kids might have some trouble putting this together, but older kids will enjoy decorating the Easer Eggs.

You'll Need:

- Paper Plate
- Tempera Paint
- Construction Paper
- Paint Brush
- Scissors
- Yarn

Directions:

1. Paint the front and back side of the paper plate with any color of tempera paint desired. Let dry.

2. Cut 6 - 9 egg shapes out of different colored paper. Punch a hole in each egg. Decorate if desired.

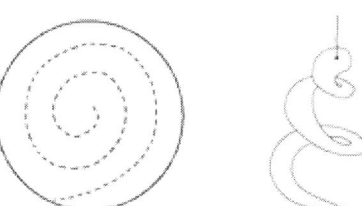

3. Cut the paper plate into a spiral as pictured below.

4. Punch one hole for each egg all the way around the outside edge of the spiral. Punch a hole in the middle of the center of the spiral.

5. Tie a piece of yarn through each egg and tie the other end of the yarn through one of the holes in the spiral. Continue with all the eggs. Tie a piece of yarn through the center hole to make a hanger.

Fish Bowl

It's good for kids to do crafts that help them think about common objects in different ways, and this fish bowl project will do the trick. Plus it's just plain fun to paint over crayons!

You'll Need:

- Paper Plate
- Blue Watercolor Paint
- Paint Brush
- Crayons
- Scissors

Directions:

1. Cut about a third of the plate off, cutting in a straight line, and discard. Cut an indent in the plate, near the flat spot, on both sides.

2. Using crayons, draw fish, plants, gravel, etc. on the back side of the plate.

3. Paint over your crayon drawing with blue watercolor paint. Let dry. The crayons will resist the paint and create a neat effect.

Don't forget to talk to kids about how the effect works -- may as well get in a little learning when you can.

Winged Ladybug

Ladybugs are a lot of fun to make, but the best ones have movable wings. This one is an easy craft to make with a paper plate that kids will love.

You'll Need:

- 2 - 9 Inch Paper Plates
- Red Tempera Paint
- Black Tempera Paint
- Paint Brush
- 2 Brads
- Black Marker
- Hole Punch
- 12 Inch Black Pipe Cleaner

Directions:

1. Paint the back side of one of the paper plates with black tempera paint. Paint the other plate with red tempera paint. Let them both dry.

2. Draw large black dots all over the red paper plate with a black marker. Cut the red plate in half.

3. Poke a brad through one corner of the red half plate into the black plate about an inch from the edge of the black plate. This is one of the ladybug wings. Do the same with the other half red plate. The two halves of the red plate should come together over the black plate and leave about an inch at the top that's not covered.

4. Punch 2 holes in the top of the black plate. Thread a black pipe cleaner in through the top of one hole and up through the bottom of the other hole to make antennas.

Simple Summer Flower

These little paper plate flowers are really cute and lots of fun to decorate. They would also make a great bulletin board decoration.

You'll Need:

- Paper Plate
- Scissors
- Green Construction Paper
- Glue
- Markers and Other Decorations

Directions:

1. Cut a paper plate as shown below.

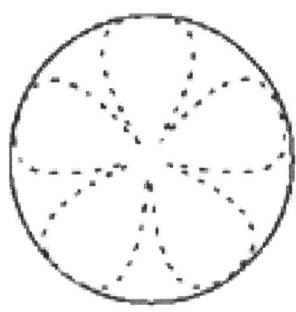

2. Cut a stem and leaves from green construction paper. Glue them to the back side of your flower so that the flower looks like it's sitting on the stem.

3. Decorate with markers, glitter, etc.

Sandy Snake

We added a little texture to the snake in this project by sprinkling some clean sand on the wet paint, but you can easily omit the sand part of the snake for a less messy project.

You'll Need:

- Paper Plate
- Green Tempera Paint
- Paint Brush
- Scissors
- Clean Sand
- Markers

Directions:

1. Spiral cut a large paper plate as shown in the diagram.

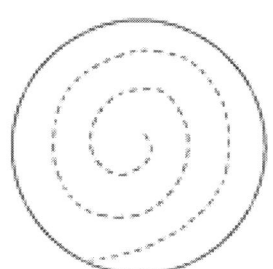

2. Paint the precut plate with green tempera paint on both sides. Sprinkle one side of the plate with sand while still wet. Let the plate dry. You may have to separate it or hang it up while it's drying so it won't stick together.

3. Draw eyes and nose holes on the head of the snake.

Monster Mask

Although we've turned this particular paper plate mask into a monster, you could easily make other kinds of masks instead. Experiment with different shapes, like a 2/3 mask, nose and mouth cutouts, or adding extra pieces to make it three dimensional.

You'll Need:

- Paper Plate
- Tempera Paint
- Paint Brush
- Markers
- Scissors
- Decorating Accessories
- Yarn or Elastic String

Directions:

1. Cut out any shape eye holes you want from a large paper plate. Put the plate up against the child's face to make sure they'll fit.

2. Paint a paper plate any color you want with tempera paint. Let dry.
3. Draw on the face with markers. Glue on other decorations like glitter, yarn, cotton balls, pom poms, buttons, etc. until you have a scary -- or not so scary -- monster mask.

4. Measure a piece of elastic thread to fit around the back of your child's head. Tie a knot in one end of a piece of elastic thread. Staple the thread to the mask on one side so that the knot is behind the staple. Do the same with the other side of the mask. The knots will keep the string from pulling loose.

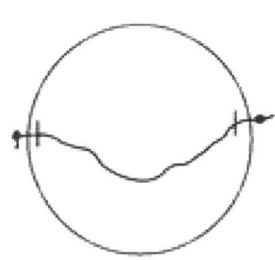

May Basket

This would make a really cute spring project or a nice gift for Mom on Mother's day. It's easy to make and looks great when it's finished!

You'll Need:

- Large Paper Plate
- Stapler
- 12 Inch Long Ribbon
- Decorating Accessories

Directions:

1. Roll the sides of a large paper plate in to the center to make a cone and staple in place.

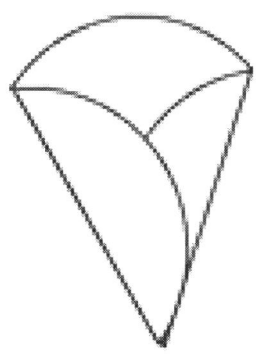

2. To make a handle, staple each end of a 12 inch piece of ribbon to either side of the cone.

3. Decorate the May basket with lace, tissue paper, ribbon, construction paper, markers, buttons, or anything you wish.

4. On May 1st, fill your cone with real, artificial, or homemade flowers and hang on the door of someone special as a May Day surprise.

Queen Of Summer Crown

Although we've made this particular crown a "girl" theme with flowers, you could easily adapt the basic idea for any theme, interest, or favorite thing. I think it would be cute to use cutouts of cars for a Kingly Crown.

You'll Need:

- Large Paper Plate
- Green Tempera Paint
- Paint Brush
- Scissors
- Construction Paper
- Glue
- Decorating Accessories

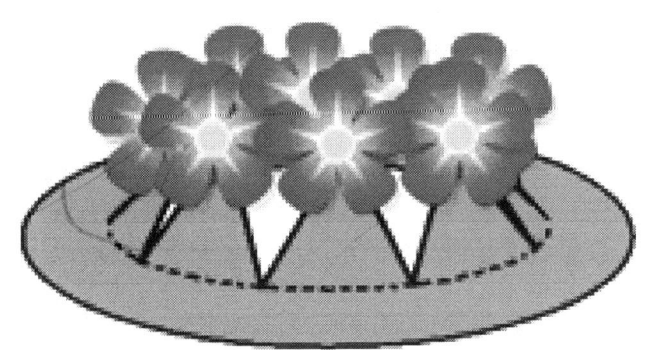

Directions:

1. Paint both sides of a paper plate with green tempera paint. Let dry.

2. Cut four slits across the center of your plate, intersecting in the center, and stopping about 1 - 2 inches from the outside of the plate. This will create eight triangles in the center of the plate.

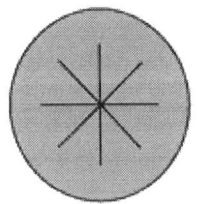 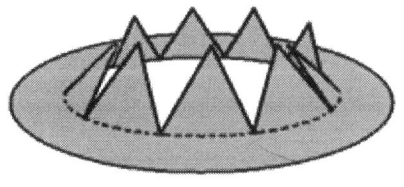

3. Bend each of the triangle center pieces up to form the crown.

4. Glue summer decorations made from construction paper onto each tip. Flowers, bees, butterflies, ice cream cones, etc. work well. You could also use stickers for this.

Door Pocket

I love it when a craft project can actually be useful too! My daughter made one of these to put all her hair accessories in, like rubber bands, hair bands, ribbons, etc. It worked like a charm and she loved it.

You'll Need:

- 2 - 9 Inch Paper Plates
- Stapler
- Markers
- Ribbon
- Hole Punch
- Decorating Accessories

Directions:

1. Cut one paper plate in half.

2. Put the whole paper plate and the half plate together with right sides together. This should create a little pocket between them. Staple them together along the edge of the half plate.

3. Punch a hole in the middle of the whole plate, at the top. Thread a piece of ribbon through the hole and tie the ends together to make a hanger.

4. Decorate the door pocket with anything you want. Markers, stickers, paper scraps, glitter, and crayons work well. When finished, slip it over a door knob and put little things inside.

> **NOTE:** I don't suggest painting these little pockets. The paint weakens the paper and it won't hold together for very long.

Advanced Techniques and Challenging Projects

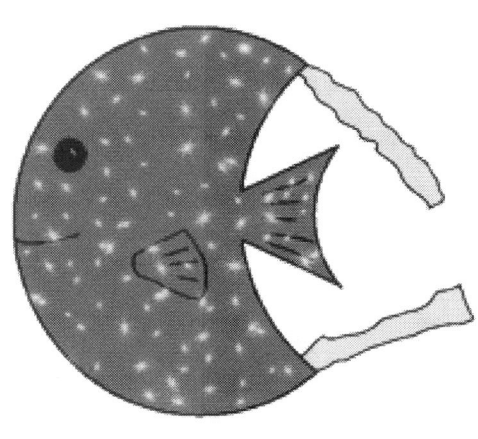

Where Do You Go From Here...

If you keep in mind all the techniques that we've discussed throughout this book, then you may be asking that question. It seems that we've probably talked about just about everything that you can possibly do with a paper plate... or have we?

Before we go any further with this chapter, let me clear one thing up right off the bat... Many of these crafts are not meant to be done with very young children. If you, or an older sibling, want to put the craft together and let a younger child help, that would probably work... if you can keep their attention. Young children won't be able to assemble many of these projects themselves.

On the other hand, some of these paper plate projects would probably be great for Girl Scouts, Boy Scouts, Summer Camp, Bible School, etc. You'll have to assess the difficulty of each idea yourself, along with the ability of your child to decide if these are right for you. Nonetheless, here are some other things you can do with a paper plate.

Combining Plates With Other Objects

You can combine paper plates with a lot of other objects to create some really great craft projects. You can also make your project a lot more challenging by combining several of the techniques we've talked about into one craft. Once you start thinking about this and start experimenting, I'm sure you'll think of some combinations that I haven't thought of.

Let's get right to the projects...

Funny Flat Elephant

This is a really cute elephant craft when you get it all put together. Be sure to let all your paint dry thoroughly before you get started or you'll have a real mess on your hands.

You'll Need:

- 2 Large Paper Plates
- 1 Small Paper Plate
- 2 Toilet Paper Tubes
- Gray Tempera Paint
- Paint Brush
- Stapler, Scissors, Glue
- Pink Construction Paper
- Black Marker

Directions:

1. Paint the back side of two large paper plates, one small paper plate, and two empty toilet paper tubes with gray tempera paint. Let dry completely.

   NOTE: If you can't find empty toilet tissue tubes, you can always use paper towel tubes and cut them to the right size for the project.

2. Cut out 2 ears, a trunk, and a tail from pink construction paper using the templates on page 52 and 53 (no tail provided).

3. Assemble the elephant according to the diagram on the next page. Lay a paper plate down on a flat surface, painted side down. Glue tail to the unpainted side of the plate, hanging out over the edge.

4. Cut each of the toilet paper tubes in half. Smash down one end of each of the half tubes and staple the flat end between the 2 plates.

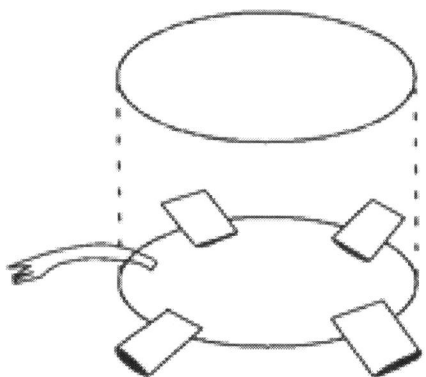

The plates should both have the painted side facing out. The tubes sticking out between the plates will be the legs.

5. Glue the ears onto the unpainted side of the small paper plate. Staple the bottom of the small plate to the front of the body between the two front legs. Glue on the trunk and draw on the eyes.

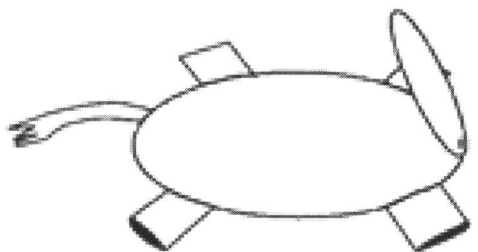

Caged Circus Animal

This would be a great project to do if you were planning a trip to the circus or the zoo!

You'll Need:

- 2 Large Paper Plates
- Red Tempera Paint
- Red Construction Paper
- Black Construction Paper
- Paint Brush
- Scissors
- Glue
- Circus Animal Picture

Directions:

1. Cut a large rectangle out of the center of one of the large paper plates. Paint the back side of that plate with red tempera paint. Let dry. This will be the front of the cage.

2. Cut a picture of a circus animal out of a magazine. Glue it to the front side of the other paper plate. You could draw an animal in if you have trouble finding a picture.

3. Staple the red plate over the unpainted plate so that the animal shows through the rectangle hole and the red side is up. Cut thin strips of red construction paper. Glue them across the rectangle to make the bars.

4. Cut two large circles of black construction paper and two small circles out of red paper. Glue the red circle to the middle of the black circle to make the wheels.

6. Glue the wheels on to the bottom of the circus cage.

Sleepy Pig

The basic construction of this pig is very similar to the elephant in this section, but it uses some different craft supplies so that you can start to get an idea of how you could use this idea to create your own animals.

You'll Need:

- 2 Large Paper Plates
- 4 Unwaxed Dixie Cups
- 1 Paper Bowl
- Pink Tempera Paint
- Pink Construction Paper
- Pink Pipe Cleaner
- Scissors
- Paint Brush
- Stapler
- Black Marker

Directions:

1. Paint the back side of the two paper plates, the back side of the paper bowl, and the four unwaxed dixie cups with pink tempera paint. Before you paint the dixie cups, take the bottoms out of them. Let dry.

2. Cut two ears, from pink construction paper (template not provided).

3. Staple the ears to the unpainted edge of the bowl (the part you eat out of) so that they stick out from the edge. This is the pig's head.

4. Assemble the pig according to the diagram below. Lay a paper plate down on a flat surface, painted side down. Staple the pink pipe cleaner tail to the unpainted side of the plate, hanging out over the edge. You can curl it around your finger.

5. Smash down the bottom end of each dixie cup and staple the flat end between the 2 plates. The plates should both have the painted side facing out. The cups sticking out between the plates will be the legs.

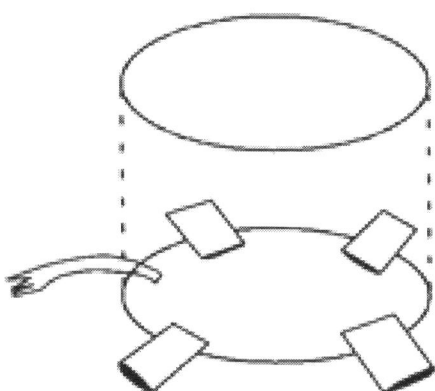

6. Fit the pig's head onto the body, between the two front legs. Staple it on the sides of the bowl where the bowl meets the plate, on the edge.

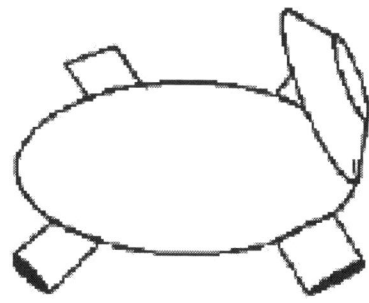

6. Draw on the pig's eyes and snout with a black marker.

Port Hole to the Ocean Floor

This is another one of those projects that's good for kids so that they learn to look at things in a different way.

You'll Need:

- 2 Large Paper Plates
- Gray Tempera Paint
- Paint Brush
- Scissors
- Stapler
- Plastic Wrap
- Transparent Tape
- Markers

Directions:

1. Cut a large circle out of the middle of one of the paper plates. Paint both sides of the plate with gray tempera paint. Let dry.

2. On the other plate, you will create a underwater scene with markers. Create your underwater scene on the front side of the plate.

3. Cut a piece of plastic wrap that's big enough to cover the hole in the gray plate. Tape it to the right side of the plate (the side of the plate you would normally eat on). This will be the "glass" separating you from the ocean as you look through your port hole.

4. Staple the two plates together so that your scene shows through the hole in the gray plate and the back side of the plate is facing you. This should create a little space between the plates.

5. Draw eight circles with a black marker to complete your port hole to the ocean floor.

Crazy Hair People

The hair on these people is a lot of fun to make, and there's a lot of variety in how they'll look based on the paper you use to make the hair.

You'll Need:

- 2 Large Paper Plates
- Tempera Paint
- Several Colors Construction Paper
- Scissors
- Paint Brush
- Markers
- Stapler

Directions:

1. Paint the back side of both paper plates any color you want. Let dry.

2. Cut several rectangles about 2 x 3 inches out of various colors of construction paper.

3. Put the two plates together with the unpainted sides together and staple once to hold them. Gather up 4 - 5 rectangles and sandwich them between the two plates, making sure that at least 2 inches of the rectangles stick out from between the plates. Staple in place. Continue all the way around the top part of the head. Try to overlap the rectangles a little. This will be the hair.

4. Cut slices into the rectangles all the way around the hair to create a fringe look. Use your hand or a pencil to roll the fringe toward the inside of the plate and separate each piece of paper. The more you mess up the hair, the better it looks.

5. Complete your crazy hair person by drawing in his face with markers.

Woven Plate

Although I've put this project in the more difficult section, this is a project that younger children can do if you cut the plate for them in advance.

You'll Need:

- Large Paper Plate
- Scissors
- Red Construction Paper
- Glue

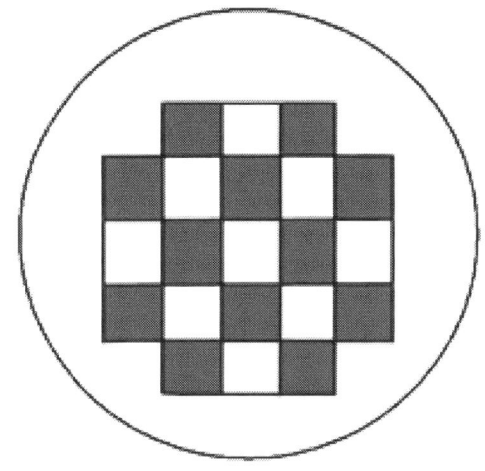

Directions:

1. Fold paper plate in half (without creasing) and cut through the center of the plate to the outside of the plate, stopping about 1 - 2 inches from the outside edge. Don't cut all the way through. Cut 6 evenly spaced slits.

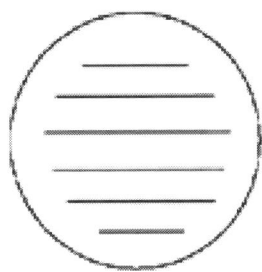

2. Cut five strips of paper that are about an inch wide and eight inches long.

3. Weave a strip of paper through the slits you made in the paper plate. Do this with the other two strips. Trim the ends if necessary and glue the ends to the back side of the plate to secure them.

Stuffed Angelfish

I love this project because I think it looks so pretty when it's finished! If you like the idea of "stuffing" paper plates, there are a lot of projects that you could adapt to use the idea.

You'll Need:

- 2 Large Paper Plates
- Scissors
- Stapler
- Newspaper
- Blue Tempera Paint
- Glitter
- Black Marker
- Streamers

Directions:

1. Cut the two paper plates according to the pattern below. Try to make them match when they are right sides together. This will be the fish body and tail.

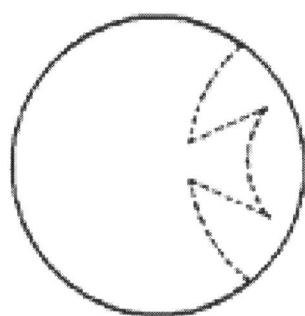

2. Out of the scraps of plate from step one, make two fins for your fish.

3. Put the two pieces of the fish body together and staple a couple of times to hold in place. Staple the rest of the way around the fish, leaving a 3 - 4 inch hole.

4. Stuff the fish with newspaper to keep it puffed out. Staple the hole shut.

5. Paint the fish with blue tempera paint. Also paint the fins you cut in step two.

6. Lightly sprinkle with glitter while the paint is still wet. Let the paint dry completely.

7. Glue the fins to both sides of the fish.

8. Draw on the eyes and mouth with a black marker.

9. Staple streamers to the sharp points on the fish near the tail. You can also staple or glue on a piece of yarn or fishing line to hang your fish if desired.

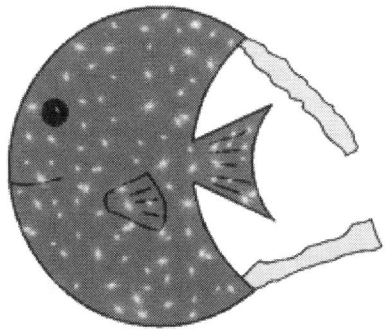

Prickly Cactus

Although I put this one in this last section of the book, it's definitely a project that younger children can do, if you draw the outline of a cactus for them on the plate. They'll love including spaghetti in their project!

You'll Need:

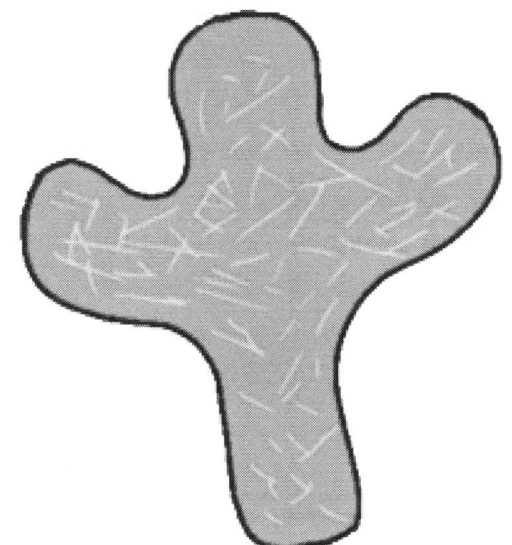

- 2 Large Paper Plates
- Green Tempera Paint
- Scissors
- Stapler
- Newspaper
- Glue
- Dry Spaghetti

Directions:

1. Cut the two paper plates into a cactus shape. Try to make them match when they are right sides together.

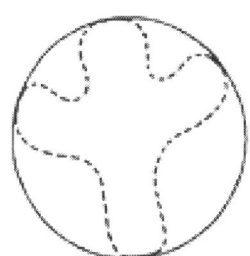

2. Staple the plates together all the way around, leaving a hole about 3 - 4 inches wide.

3. Stuff the cactus with newspaper. Staple the hole shut.

4. Paint both sides of the cactus with green tempera paint. Let dry.

5. Break up several pieces of dry spaghetti into smaller pieces. Glue them on the cactus to make it prickly.

Rocking on the Sea

I've included this project to give you more ideas on the different kinds of projects you can make with paper plates. Hopefully it will spark your own unique ideas!

You'll Need:

- Large Paper Plate
- Blue Watercolor Paint
- Paint Brush
- Heavy Brown Construction Paper
- Red and White Construction Paper
- Scissors
- Blue Marker
- Glue

Directions:

1. Paint both sides of a large paper plate with blue watercolor paint. Let dry. Fold the plate in half and crease it.

2. Cut a rectangle that's four inches long and half an inch wide out of heavy brown construction paper or cardboard to make the mast.

Fold it in half lengthwise. Cut a slit in the rectangle, along the fold, about an inch long and on one end of the rectangle.

Slip the rectangle over the fold in the paper plate on the slit end so that an inch of the end of the rectangle is on both sides of the plate. Glue in place.

3. Cut out two boat shapes from red construction paper. (A hexagon cut in half works well.) Glue one boat onto each side of the fold on the paper plate.

Make sure the top of the boat is even with the fold on the plate and that it covers the ends of the mast that you glued to the plate.

4. Cut two identical right triangles from white construction paper. Glue them together over the mast so that the mast is sandwiched between the triangles. This makes the sail.

5. With a blue marker, draw the waves on the ocean on both sides of the fold. Slightly unfold your plate. Set your boat up on the rounded side and let it rock back and forth.

   Note: Although this project may seem a little complicated when you're reading it, it will make sense when you're actually making it.

Coming Soon...

Little Kid Best Loved Book Activities
Crafts, Recipes, and Learning Activities Based on
50 Popular and Award Winning Children's Books

****

Little Kid Christmas Crafts

****

Crafty Concoctions for Little Kids
Recipes and Instructions for Homemade
Art and Craft Supplies and How To Use Them

****

Little Kid Seuss Theme Activities
Crafts, Recipes, and Learning Activities Based on
The Most Popular and Loved Dr. Seuss Books

****

Little Kid Halloween Crafts

****

Little Kid Edible Art
Recipes That Kids Love to Make, Eat, and Create With

Made in the USA
Middletown, DE
12 June 2019